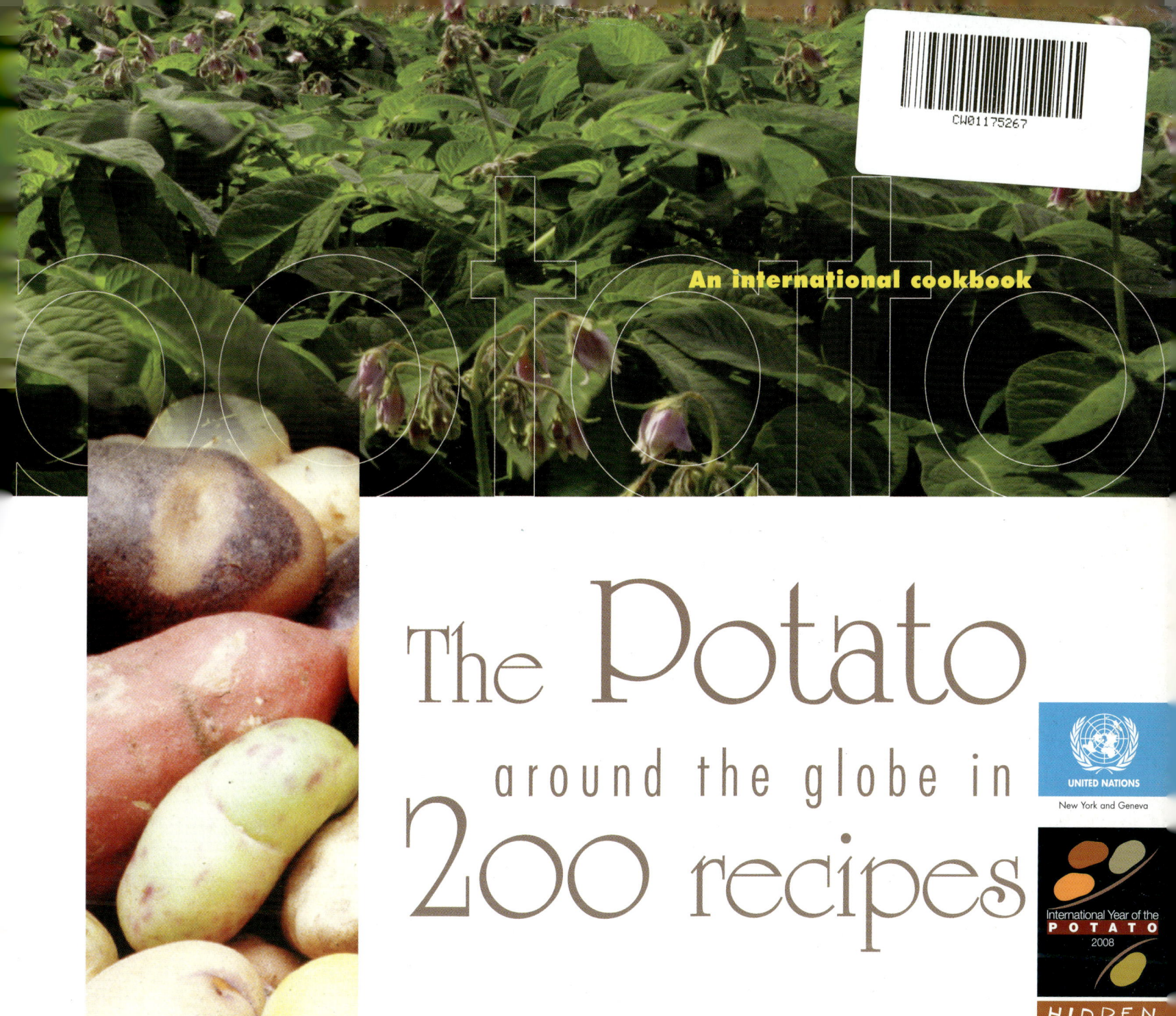

An international cookbook

The Potato
around the globe in 200 recipes

Recipes collected by Florence Lebras

UNITED NATIONS
New York and Geneva

International Year of the POTATO 2008

HIDDEN TREASURE

Foreword

One of the essential roles of the United Nations Economic Commission for Europe (UNECE) is to promote international trade in order not only to improve our standard of living but also to promote stability and peace in this region.

To facilitate exchanges and to protect consumers, UNECE has developed a series of norms and standards in particular for transport and trade, but also for agricultural products.

At the beginning of the 1950s the member States of UNECE asked the Commission to establish quality standards for agricultural products which were exchanged throughout the region. These standards deal with fresh fruit and vegetables, dry and dried products, seed potatoes, early and ware potatoes, meat, cut flowers and eggs exported or imported by the 56 member countries of UNECE. These standards help in facilitating international trade, and they also encourage the production of quality goods, improve the profitability of producers and protect consumers' interests.

Among these standards, those on potatoes are of special importance this year since the United Nations General Assembly at its sixtieth session declared 2008 to be the International Year of the Potato. It has affirmed "the need to focus world attention on the role that the potato can play in providing food security and eradicating poverty in support of achievement of the internationally agreed development goals, including the Millennium Development Goals" and has invited all relevant organizations of the United Nations system to actively participate in this celebration.

This cookbook prepared by UNECE aims not only to show that potatoes are used by a wide range of countries throughout the world, but also to attract the attention of consumers to the importance of the quality standards elaborated by the UNECE. Indeed, in addition to the recipes, good quality produce is indispensable for preparing these delicious dishes.

Marek Belka
United Nations Under-Secretary-General
Executive Secretary of the United Nations Economic Commission for Europe

Foreword

The "hidden treasure", the potato, is the world's fourth most important food, after maize, wheat and rice. For millennia it has been the staple food of a large part of the world's population.

Although introduced into Europe and North America less than five hundred years ago, DNA research indicates that potatoes were being cultivated in South America near Lake Titicaca in the Andes already some 8,000 years ago. Latin America today boasts over 4,000 varieties of potato.

The potato is also one of the world's healthiest root vegetables, with a larger high-quality protein content than that of other roots and tubers. And it's a valuable source of vitamins, minerals and fibre. A single medium-sized potato, for instance, provides you with nearly half the daily adult requirement of vitamin C. The nutrient-rich potato can contribute to improved diets, thus reducing mortality rates caused by malnutrition.

The United Nations has proclaimed 2008 the International Year of the Potato to raise the profile of this globally important food crop and commodity. The Year will also highlight the biological and nutritional attributes of the potato, and promote its production, processing, consumption, marketing and trade.

At the United Nations Economic Commission for Europe, a group of specialists of which I am currently the chairperson, deals with standardizing the quality of seed potatoes for international trade. We work towards ensuring that only healthy and high-yielding seed potatoes enter the international market. We meet at least once a year to discuss and if necessary update the seed-potato standard.

I hope that this attractively produced book will introduce you to new and exciting ways to delight your palate and impress your friends. Good luck in preparing your dishes of this "hidden treasure", the potato. And bon appétit!

Pier Giacomo Bianchi
Chairperson
Specialized Section on the Standardization of Seed Potatoes
United Nations Economic Commission for Europe

Foreword

The humble potato holds enormous promise to contribute to meeting the food needs of the developing world. In fact, the adjective "humble" is a complete misnomer. Potatoes are the world's most important root and tuber crop and the fourth most important food crop, after rice, maize, and wheat. Today, potatoes are grown in over 130 countries throughout the world and over a billion people eat them daily.

The United Nations declared 2008 the International Year of the Potato, noting that the potato is a staple food in the diet of the world's population. It affirms the need to focus world attention on the role that the potato can play in providing food security and eradicating poverty, an overarching development goal of the United Nations as stated in the Millennium Declaration adopted by the international community on the eve of the twenty-first century.

In ancient Peru, potatoes were a valuable source of food that freed the Andean peoples from hunger. The potato yields more nutritious food more quickly on less land and in harsher climates than any other major crop. Potatoes produce more food per unit of water than any other major crop. They are also delicious, and far from being fattening, a medium-sized potato boiled with the skin on provides about 100 calories, 26 grams of carbohydrates, zero cholesterol, about 4 grams of protein, 3 grams of fibre, about half the daily adult requirement of vitamin C, as well as significant amounts of iron, potassium, zinc, thiamin, niacin and vitamin B6.

Nowadays, almost 5,000 varieties of potato exist, with a fantastic range of shapes, sizes, flavours and colours, from pure white to deep purple. There are thousands of ways to cook them. With its delicious recipes, I am sure that this cookbook will introduce more people to the delights of the potato.

The potato has come a long way since it was blamed for causing everything from lust to leprosy. I firmly believe that this healthy tuber will increasingly play a vital role in alleviating hunger and improving the livelihoods and health of different populations around the world.

Dr Pamela K. Anderson
Director General
International Potato Center (CIP)
Lima - Peru

Acknowledgements

All our thanks to Florence Lebras who collected the recipes and without whom this book would never have come to life. To Nathalie Quint, Joumana Nehme, Barbara Casassus, Annemie Schmidt, Stéphanie Smith, who provided some of the recipes. To Amélie Churlet and Yuliya Skorobogatova, for the potato anecdotes. To the International Potato Center (Lima, Peru) and Sue Gilbert (United Kingdom) for the photographs. Special thanks to Kate Mangin for all her work on the English version as well as to all the production team of the United Nations Office at Geneva.

Jean Michel Jakobowicz

Former Chief of the Information Unit,
United Nations Economic Commission for Europe

DRY MEASURES

Metric	Imperial / US
15 g	1/2 oz
30 g	1 oz
60 g	2 oz
90 g	3 oz
115 g	4 oz (¼lb)
140 g	5 oz
170 g	6 oz
200 g	7 oz
230 g	8 oz (½lb)
260 g	9 oz
290 g	10 oz
315 g	11 oz
340 g	12 oz (¾lb)
370 g	13 oz
400 g	14 oz
430 g	15 oz
450 g	16 oz (1lb)
680 g	24 oz (1½ lb)
900 g	32 oz (2lb)
1 kg	35 oz

LIQUID MEASURES

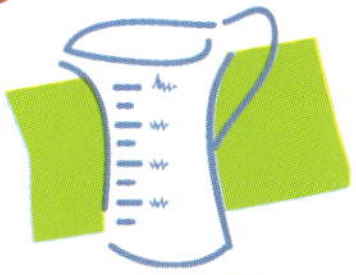

Metric	Imperial / US	US
15 ml	1/2 fluid oz	1 level tbsp
30 ml	1 fl oz	1/8 cup
60 ml	2 fl oz	1/4 cup
90 ml	3 fl oz	3/8 cup
120 ml	4 fl oz	1/2 cup
150 ml	5 fl oz/¼ pint	2/3 cup
180 ml	6 fl oz	3/4 cup
240 ml	8 fl oz	1 cup
300 ml	10 fl oz/½ pint	1 ¼ cups
360 ml	12 fl oz	1 ½ cups
500 ml	16 fl oz	2 cups
600 ml	20 fl oz/1 pint	2 ½ cups/1 US pint
750 ml	1 ½ pints	3 ¾ cups
1000 ml/1 litre	1 ¾ pints	4 cups/1 quart

ABBREVIATIONS

Kilogram .... kg
Gram .... g
Ounce .... oz
Pound .... lb
Litre l
Decilitre .... dl
Centilitre cl
Millilitre .... ml
Teaspoon .... tsp
Tablespoon ..... tbsp

OVEN TEMPERATURES

C° (Celsius)	F° (Fahrenheit)	Gas Mark
110	225	¼
120	250	½
140	275	1
150	300	2
160	325	3
180	350	4
190	375	5
200	400	6
220	425	7
230	450	8

2oo recipes

Boranie katschalu

 **Preparation time**
15 minutes

 **Cooking time**
35 minutes

 **Serves** 4

 **Difficulty** Easy

Ingredients

1 kg potatoes
4 onions, peeled and chopped
150g fromage blanc
2 garlic cloves, peeled and chopped
60ml oil
1 teaspoon ground coriander
2 tablespoons tomato concentrate
½ teaspoon curry powder
½ teaspoon cayenne pepper
4 sprigs of mint, chopped
salt

Preparation

Peel and wash the potatoes, dry them and cut into rounds.

Place the tomato concentrate and spices in a bowl and add 100ml water.

Heat the oil in a large frying pan and cook the onion for 5 minutes over a low heat to soften, then add the potatoes. Brown them for 5 minutes, then add the mixture from the bowl. Add 250ml water, salt and pepper, cover and leave to simmer for 20 minutes.

Combine the garlic with the fromage blanc. Spread half of it in a serving dish, cover with potatoes, and add the rest of the fromage blanc.

Garnish with the chopped mint.

Afghanistan

Katschalu e joschdaada

 **Preparation time**
15 minutes

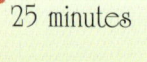 **Cooking time**
25 minutes

 **Serves** 4

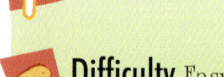 **Difficulty** Easy

Ingredients

1 kg potatoes
2 chillies, seeded
1 bunch of coriander, chopped
juice of 1 lemon
6 tablespoons oil
salt and pepper

Preparation

Cook the unpeeled potatoes for 25 minutes, set aside to cool, then peel them, cut them into rounds and place them in a salad bowl.

Put the chillies, lemon juice and coriander in a food processor and whiz. Add salt, pepper and the oil, pour over the potatoes and mix together.

Serve cold.

Afghanistan

Khorme katschalu

Preparation time
10 minutes

Cooking time
35 minutes

Serves 4

Difficulty Easy

Ingredients

1 kg potatoes

4 onions, peeled and diced

1 tablespoon tomato concentrate

½ teaspoon curry powder

2 pinches of cayenne pepper

200ml oil

salt and pepper

Preparation

Peel and wash the potatoes, dry them and cut into chunks.

Heat the oil in a frying pan and brown the onions for 5 minutes, stirring all the time. Add the potatoes and brown for 5 minutes, then add the tomato concentrate, spices and 350ml water. Mix well, add salt and pepper. Cover and leave to simmer for 25 minutes.

Serve hot.

Afghanistan

Pakavre katschalu

Preparation time
15 minutes

Cooking time
10 minutes

Serves 4

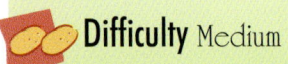
Difficulty Medium

Ingredients
4 large potatoes
200g chick pea flour
10g baking powder
½ teaspoon dried yeast
1tsp curry powder
oil for deep frying
salt

Preparation

Peel and wash the potatoes, dry them and cut into thin rounds. Place them in a large bowl and cover with water.

Put 250ml water in a jug, add the curry powder, a pinch of salt and the baking powder.

Mix together the flour and yeast in a bowl and slowly add the water, mixing well to obtain a creamy batter. Set aside for 20 minutes.

Heat the frying oil. Dip the potato rounds into the batter and then deep fry them. Remove them from the oil as soon as they are browned, drain on kitchen paper.

Fry the potato rounds in batches so the oil doesn't cool too much.

Afghanistan

Potato patties with coriander

Preparation time
20 minutes

Cooking time
30 minutes

Serves 4

Difficulty Easy

Ingredients

800g potatoes
3 eggs, beaten
1 tablespoon paprika
2 teaspoons ground cumin
bunch of fresh coriander, chopped
salt, cayenne pepper

Preparation

Peel the potatoes, steam or cook in boiling salted water for 20 minutes. Drain and mash them. Add the paprika, cumin, eggs, salt, cayenne pepper and mix together.

Spread the mixture on a lightly floured surface and cut out rounds of about 12cm diameter. Set aside in refrigerator for 30 minutes.

Heat the oil in a large frying pan. Fry the patties until golden brown on both sides. Drain on kitchen paper.

Algeria

Potatoes stuffed with sardines

Preparation time
15 minutes

Cooking time
40 minutes

Serves 4

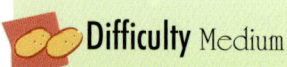
Difficulty Medium

Ingredients
1 kg sardines
1 kg potatoes
2 onions, peeled and chopped
25g butter
6 tablespoons olive oil
a bunch of parsley
500ml vegetable stock
salt and pepper
1 teaspoon ground cinnamon

Algeria

Preparation

Peel the potatoes, cut them in half lengthways and scoop out the centre with a spoon. Steam or cook in boiling salted water for 20 minutes and drain.

Remove the backbone and skin from the sardines. Put the fillets in a bowl and add the butter, salt, pepper and cinnamon. Mix thoroughly.

In a large pan, fry the onions in the olive oil, season with salt, pepper and cinnamon. Add the stock.

Spoon the mixture into the potato cases and place them in the onion sauce, with the open side facing upwards. Cover and leave to cook for about 15 minutes.

Serve hot.

Ocro criollo (Beef, potato and corn stew)

Preparation time
35 minutes

Cooking time
5 hours

Serves 6

Difficulty Easy

Ingredients
300g potatoes
300g sweet potatoes
300g white beans (soaked the day before)
300g white cabbage
300g sweetcorn
300g pumpkin
300g carrots, peeled
200g bacon
3 sausages, thickly sliced
3 chorizos, thickly sliced
300g loin of pork, diced
300g veal, diced
300g beef, diced

For the sauce:
10 garlic cloves, peeled and chopped
2 shallots, peeled and chopped
200ml oil
salt and pepper
chilli powder

Preparation

Put the water in which the beans have been soaking into a stewpot, add the beans, sausages and meats. Bring to the boil, then lower the heat and leave to simmer for 4 hours, stirring from time to time.

Peel all the vegetables and dice them. Add them, together with the sweetcorn, to the stewpot and cook for 1 hour.

For the sauce: Combine the garlic and shallots with the oil, salt, pepper and chilli powder.

This is a traditional dish from the north of Argentina.

Argentina

Potato cake

 **Preparation time**
45 minutes

 **Cooking time**
40 minutes

 **Serves** 4 to 6

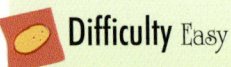 **Difficulty** Easy

Ingredients

For the pastry:
300g flour
60g lard, softened
salt

For the filling:
1 kg potatoes
750g beef, diced
6 eggs + 2 egg yolks
3 onions, peeled and chopped
100g stoned black olives
100g grated parmesan cheese
3 tablespoons olive oil
½ teaspoon paprika
2 teaspoons ground cinnamon
salt, pepper, sugar

Argentina

Preparation

Place the flour on a work surface. Make a well and add a large pinch of salt, the softened lard and 100ml cold water. Knead together to form a soft dough. Cover with a cloth and chill.

Hard-boil 4 of the eggs, peel and chop them.

Heat the olive oil in a pan. Cook the meat and onions for 5 minutes, stirring all the time. Add salt and pepper, and sprinkle with paprika. Set aside to cool.

When the mixture is cool add the hard-boiled eggs and the olives.

Steam or boil the unpeeled potatoes for 25 minutes, peel and mash them, and season with salt and pepper. Add the butter, parmesan, and the 2 remaining whole eggs, beaten.

Preheat the oven to 180°C.

Line a deep flan dish with the pastry. Spoon in the meat mixture and spread the potatoes on top. Brush with the remaining 2 egg yolks, sprinkle with sugar and cinnamon and bake in the oven for 45 minutes.

Serve hot.

This is one of the oldest recipes of South America.

Hachlama

Preparation time
10 minutes

Cooking time
2 hours

Serves 4

Difficulty Easy

Ingredients

500g potatoes peeled and chopped

800g shoulder of lamb, cut into chunks

2 carrots, peeled and chopped

3 tomatoes, chopped

1 stick of celery, washed, trimmed and diced

1 tablespoon paprika

salt

Preparation

Place the meat in a stewpot, cover with water and bring to the boil. Skim, then lower the heat, cover with a lid and leave to simmer for 1 hour.

Add the vegetables, paprika and a little salt. Cover and cook for another 45 minutes.

Serve hot.

Armenia

Potato keuftés

Preparation time
25 minutes

Cooking time
35 minutes

Serves 4

Difficulty Medium

Ingredients

800g potatoes
250g minced meat, cooked
2 eggs
oil for deep frying
1 tablespoon flour
salt and pepper

Armenia

Preparation

Steam or boil the unpeeled potatoes for 25 minutes, drain, peel and mash them. Stir in the flour, and one of the eggs, beaten. Add salt and pepper.

Form balls the size of an egg, dig a small hole in the centre of each and fill it with meat. Close the potato around the meat so that it is completely covered.

Beat the remaining egg in a bowl.

Heat the frying oil. Dip the balls into the beaten egg and deep fry them until golden brown. Drain on kitchen paper.

Serve hot.

Topic

Preparation time
30 minutes

Cooking time
1 hour 20 minutes

Serves 6

Difficulty Medium

Ingredients

600g potatoes

600g chick peas (put to soak the day before)

For the stuffing:

2kg onions, peeled and chopped

3 tablespoons pine nuts

3 tablespoons currants

200g tahini

1 tablespoon cumin

1tsp Jamaica pepper

salt

To serve:

cinnamon

olive oil

lemon juice

Preparation

Cook the chick peas in boiling water for 30 minutes. Peel and wash the potatoes, cut them into chunks and steam or cook in boiling water for 25 minutes.

Drain the potatoes and chick peas and mash them.

Put the onions in a pan and cover with water. Bring to the boil and cook for 10 minutes. When the water has evaporated, add the pine nuts, currants, cumin, pepper, tahini and a pinch of salt. Mix well.

Cut out 12 squares of gauze and dampen them. In the middle of each put 3 tablespoons of the mashed vegetables and flatten them down. Add a little onion mixture in the centre and fold the gauze over the stuffing. Knot the ends of the gauze so that the balls are enclosed in it.

Bring some salted water to the boil, drop in the gauze bundles and cook for 20 minutes. Remove them carefully, leave them to drain and cool.

Serve with cinnamon, olive oil and lemon juice.

Tahini is a paste based on sesame seeds which you can find in specialist grocery stores.

Armenia

Potato scallops

 **Preparation time**
20 minutes

 **Cooking time**
15 minutes

 **Serves** 4

 **Difficulty** Easy

Ingredients

1 kg potatoes
1 tablespoon plain flour
100g self-raising flour
oil for deep frying
salt

Preparation

Wash and peel the potatoes, dry them and cut into slices about 2mm thick.

Put the sliced potatoes into a bowl filled with cold water and let them soak for 30 minutes. Drain and dry thoroughly on kitchen paper – they should be as dry as possible.

Put both types of flour into a large bowl, add 250ml water and beat with a fork until the mixture is frothy.

Heat the oil in a deep fryer or a large pan. Drop the potato slices into the flour, then fry until they are golden brown and tender. Remove using a slotted spoon and drain them on kitchen paper before placing them in a serving dish. Add salt just before serving.

Australia

Kartoffelsuppe – (Potato soup)

Preparation time
15 minutes

Cooking time
35 minutes

Serves 6

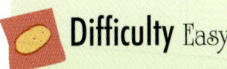
Difficulty Easy

Ingredients

600g potatoes, peeled and diced

1 medium onion, peeled and chopped

1 leek, trimmed, washed and chopped

500ml milk

25g butter

4 sprigs of parsley

½ bunch of chives

1 egg yolk

3 tablespoons crème fraîche

salt and pepper

For the garnish:
6 tablespoons flour
1 egg

Preparation

Combine the flour and whole egg until they form a compact dough. Grate the dough with a large grater and set aside to dry.

Peel and chop the potatoes into small pieces. Place the potatoes, onion and leek in a large pan and cover with a litre of water. Bring to the boil and cook for 30 minutes. Blend the mixture and return it to the pan. Add the milk, salt and pepper and continue cooking for 5 minutes.

Remove the pan from the heat and add the butter.

In a small bowl combine the egg yolk and crème fraîche with 2 tablespoons of the soup. Add it to the pan. Mix well and garnish with the grated dough.

Austria

Potato salad with radishes

 **Preparation time**
15 minutes

 Cooking time
20 minutes

 Serves 4

 Difficulty Easy

Ingredients

800g potatoes
250ml vegetable stock
1 teaspoon mustard
2 tablespoons vinegar
1 teaspoon olive oil
4 gherkins, sliced
15 radishes, sliced
2 sprigs of parsley, chopped

Preparation

Pour the stock into a saucepan, add the mustard and stir well.

Peel the potatoes, cut them into slices and add them to the stock. Bring to the boil and cook for about 15 minutes. Remove the potato slices from the pan and place in a bowl, leaving about 6 or 7 slices in the stock.

Mash the potato slices left in the pan with the stock, add the vinegar and oil and pour over the potato slices.

Sprinkle the radishes, gherkins and parsley over the salad.

Serve warm.

The potato was imported from Latin America. However, it was not well received by the Europeans. The Scots at one time refused to eat potatoes because they were not mentioned in the Bible. On the other hand in the Andes, the Incas thought potatoes made childbirth easier and used them to treat injuries.

Austria

Salzburg potatoes

Preparation time
40 minutes

Cooking time
35 minutes

Serves 4

Difficulty Easy

Ingredients

4 large potatoes

100g ham, diced

1 onion, peeled and chopped

1 egg yolk

2 tablespoons flour

50g butter

500ml milk

2 tablespoons cream

4 tablespoons breadcrumbs

salt, pepper, nutmeg

Preparation

Steam or boil the unpeeled potatoes for 30 minutes. Cut the top off each potato and scoop out the pulp, taking care not to pierce the outer skin.

Mash the pulp and add the cream, egg yolk, a pinch of salt, pepper and nutmeg. Add the onion and ham to the potato and mix together well.

Spoon the mixture into the potato cases and arrange them in an ovenproof dish.

Melt the butter in a small saucepan, sprinkle on the flour and add the milk a little at a time, stirring all the time.

When the sauce coats the back of the spoon remove from the heat. Pour the sauce over the potatoes and sprinkle with breadcrumbs. Brown under a grill for 5 minutes.

Austria

What is a potato exactly?

The potato is a tuber, which means that it is neither a fruit, nor a bulb, nor a subterranean fruit, but simply part of an underground stem which continues to live, breathe, consume, transform and propagate before it finally shrivels up and dies.

Draniki

**Preparation time**
20 minutes

**Cooking time**
20 minutes

**Serves** 4

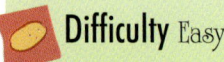**Difficulty** Easy

Ingredients
12 medium-sized potatoes
1 egg, beaten
2 tablespoons flour
8 tablespoons vegetable oil
250ml sour cream
salt

Belarus

Preparation

Wash and peel the potatoes. Dry them well and grate coarsely.

Mix the potatoes with the flour, beaten egg, cream and a little salt. Form into small pancakes about 10cm in diameter.

Heat the oil in a large pan. Fry the pancakes until golden brown and crispy on both sides. Drain them on kitchen paper.

Serve hot with sour cream.

If you can't find sour cream, mix the juice of a lemon with 300ml cream.

Dratcena

Preparation time
15 minutes

Cooking time
40 minutes

Serves 4

Difficulty Easy

Ingredients

6 potatoes, grated
2 onions, peeled and chopped
250g smoked bacon bits
30g butter
salt and pepper

Preparation

Peel and wash the potatoes. Dry them and grate into a bowl.

Fry the onions and bacon, then add them to the grated potatoes, season with salt and pepper.

Preheat the oven to 180° C.

Transfer the mixture to a buttered gratin dish and bake in the oven for 30 minutes.

Serve hot.

Belarus

Kardoupliniki

 **Preparation time**
20 minutes

 **Cooking time**
30 minutes

 **Serves** 4

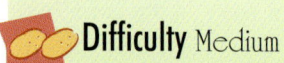 **Difficulty** Medium

Ingredients

8 potatoes, peeled and cut into pieces
250g tin of chopped white mushrooms
1 onion, peeled and chopped
1 egg, beaten
100ml milk
20g butter
oil for deep frying
salt and pepper

Belarus

Preparation

Steam or boil the potatoes for 20 minutes, drain and mash them. Add salt, pepper and the milk, stir well.

Brown the onion with the mushrooms in a knob of butter.

Divide the mashed potatoes into 8 parts and form each into a flattened pasty. Spoon some of the onion and mushroom mixture into the middle of each. Fold in half to cover the filling and pinch the edges firmly to seal.

Brush the pasties with beaten egg.

Heat the frying oil and fry until golden brown.

Fried potatoes

Preparation time
10 minutes

Cooking time
15 minutes

Serves 4

Difficulty Easy

Ingredients

1 kg potatoes
oil for deep frying
salt

Preparation

Peel the potatoes and cut into sticks about 1cm thick. Rinse and dry thoroughly.

Heat the oil to 160°C. Plunge the potato sticks into the hot oil and deep fry 5 minutes. The sticks should rise to the surface. Remove and drain on kitchen paper. Leave them to cool down.

Reheat the oil to 180°C, then plunge sticks into the oil and cook for 5 minutes.

Drain well, put in a dish and sprinkle with salt.

Serve hot.

Belgium

In Belgium, fried potatoes are traditionally served with mussels.

Liégeois potatoes

Preparation time
15 minutes

Cooking time
55 minutes

Serves 4

Difficulty Easy

Ingredients

800g potatoes
400g green beans
200g bacon, cut into strips
1 onion, peeled and chopped
20g butter
3 sprigs fresh tarragon, chopped
2 tablespoons vinegar
salt

Preparation

Steam or boil the unpeeled potatoes for 30 minutes. Peel and slice them across, put aside and keep warm.

Trim the beans and cook for 12-15 minutes in boiling salted water. Drain and keep warm.

Fry the bacon in a pan with the butter, add the onion and continue cooking for 5 minutes. Deglaze the pan with vinegar.

Place the potatoes and beans in a shallow dish, add the onions and bacon, pour the sauce over the top and sprinkle with tarragon.

Serve hot.

Potato and bacon chicory

Preparation time
10 minutes

Cooking time
30 minutes

Serves 4

Difficulty Easy

Ingredients

600g potatoes
6 heads of chicory
250g smoked bacon bits
2 tablespoons wine vinegar
salt and pepper

Preparation

Steam or boil the unpeeled potatoes for 20 minutes, peel them and cut into small cubes.

Wash the chicory, trim the bases, core and chop finely.

Dry fry (without oil or fat) the bacon bits in a pan, deglaze with the vinegar.

Preheat the oven to 180°C.

In an oven dish mix together the potatoes, chicories and bacon, add pepper and a little salt.

Heat in the oven for 10 minutes.

Serve this dish with a pork roast.

Belgium

Potatoes à l'ardennaise

Preparation time
15 minutes

Cooking time
45 minutes

Serves 4

Difficulty Easy

Ingredients

6 potatoes
2 turnips
4 carrots
2 leeks (white part only)
1 onion
2 garlic cloves
2 sticks of celery
4 pork chops
100g smoked bacon bits
2 tablespoons flour
50g butter
1 sprig of thyme
1 bay leaf
salt and pepper

Belgium

Preparation

Peel and dice the carrots, turnips, onion, garlic, celery and leeks.

Melt 25g butter in a frying pan, brown the onion and garlic for 3 minutes stirring all the time, then add the celery, carrots, leeks, and turnips. Stir and cover with hot water. Add salt, pepper, thyme and the bay leaf, cover and leave to cook for 20 minutes on a low heat.

Peel and wash the potatoes and cut them into cubes.

Coat the bacon bits with flour and brown them in the rest of the butter in a pan. Add the pork chops and brown them on both sides.

Pour the vegetables and the stock over the meat, add the potatoes. Cover and cook over a low heat for 15 minutes.

Stoemp with Brussels sprouts

Preparation time
20 minutes

Cooking time
60 minutes

Serves 4 to 6

Difficulty Easy

Ingredients

1 kg potatoes
500g Brussels sprouts, halved
250g carrots, peeled and chopped
250g leeks, trimmed, washed and cut in thin strips
1 onion, peeled and chopped
250g bacon, cut in strips
100g butter
100ml milk
2 sprigs parsley, chopped
salt and pepper

Preparation

Steam or boil the unpeeled potatoes for 25 minutes.

Melt the butter in a frying pan, add the carrots, onion, sprouts and leeks. Brown the vegetables for 10 minutes, stirring often. Cover with cold water, and season with salt and pepper. Cover the pan and leave to simmer for 30 minutes.

Fry the bacon in a pan until golden brown.

Peel and mash the potatoes, then add the milk a little at a time while whisking.

Transfer the potatoes to a serving dish, add the vegetables and bacon.

Sprinkle with the parsley and serve hot.

Belgium

Sweet potato pudding

Preparation time
15 minutes

Cooking time
45 minutes

Serves 10

Difficulty Easy

Ingredients

800g sweet potatoes
200g sugar
1 tablespoon powdered vanilla
2 tablespoons grated ginger
125g butter
300ml coconut milk
30ml condensed milk
4 tablespoons raisins

Belize

Preparation

Preheat the oven to 180°C.

Peel the sweet potatoes and grate them into a bowl. Add the sugar and the coconut milk and mix together until the sugar is dissolved.

Add the butter and condensed milk, then the vanilla, ginger and raisins.

Combine until smooth, then pour into an oven dish

Bake in the oven for 45 minutes.

Leave to cool.

Sailors often ate potatoes on board ship to prevent scurvy, a disease caused by vitamin C deficiency.

Saltenas

Preparation time
25 minutes

Cooking time
50 minutes

Serves 4 to 6

Difficulty Easy

Ingredients

4 potatoes
4 onions, peeled and roughly chopped
250g green beans
500g cooked chicken breast, diced
25g margarine
½ tablespoon cumin
½ tablespoon oregano
4 hard-boiled eggs, sliced
2 tablespoons raisins
2 tablespoons stoned black olives
4 sprigs of parsley, chopped
1 packet ready-made shortcrust pastry
salt

Preparation

Peel the potatoes, steam or cook them in boiling salted water for 25 minutes, drain and dice.

Steam or boil the green beans for 10 minutes, cut into small lengths.

In a bowl mix together the vegetables, parsley, chicken, olives, raisins and spices.

Roll out the pastry on a lightly floured surface and cut out rounds. Spoon some stuffing into the centre of each together with a slice of egg. Fold the pasties in half to cover the filling and pinch the edges firmly to seal.

Preheat the oven to 180°C.

Melt the margarine and brush it over the pasties.

Arrange them in a gratin dish and cook in the oven for 15 minutes.

Serve hot or warm.

Bolivia

Pura - (Bosnia)

Preparation time
15 minutes

Cooking time
30 minutes

Serves 4

Difficulty Easy

Ingredients

6 potatoes, peeled and cut in small pieces
500g polenta
10 garlic cloves, peeled and crushed
4 Greek-style yoghurts
50g butter
Salt

Preparation

Peel the potatoes and cut them into small chunks. Cover them with water, add salt and cook for 20 minutes.

Add the polenta to the pan and continue cooking on a low heat until all the water is absorbed. Transfer to a serving dish.

Mix the yoghurts with the crushed garlic, add salt and stir well.

Melt the butter in a pan and pour it over the potatoes.

Pour the yoghurt sauce over the dish before serving.

This dish is prepared in all Bosnian families, who all have their own way of making it.

Potato and Jerusalem artichoke cream

Preparation time
15 minutes

Cooking time
20 minutes

Serves 4

Difficulty Easy

Ingredients

4 potatoes
3 Jerusalem artichokes
2 leeks, trimmed and washed
1 garlic clove, peeled and chopped
3cm piece of root ginger, peeled and grated
1 litre chicken stock
3 tablespoons cream
2 spring onions, peeled and finely chopped
salt and pepper

Preparation

Peel the potatoes, leeks and Jerusalem artichokes and cut them into chunks.

Put the chicken stock in a large pan. Add the vegetables, garlic and ginger. Cover and leave to simmer for 20 minutes.

Liquidise the soup and transfer it to a soup tureen. Add salt and pepper to taste, and stir in the cream.

Garnish with the onions before serving.

Brazil

Salpicão facil

Preparation time
15 minutes

Cooking time
25 minutes

Serves 4

Difficulty Easy

Ingredients

4 potatoes
4 carrots, peeled and grated
1 green pepper, skinned, seeded and diced
1 red pepper, skinned, seeded and diced
2 onions, peeled and chopped
500g chicken breast, diced
1 tin of peas, strained
125g mayonnaise
juice of 1 lemon
4 sprigs of parsley, chopped

Preparation

Steam or boil the unpeeled potatoes for 25 minutes, peel and dice them.

Put all the vegetables and chicken in a salad bowl.

Add the lemon juice and parsley to the mayonnaise.

Pour it over the salad, stir and serve cold.

Brazil

To peel peppers easily, use a potato peeler. Or grill them, turning them over and over; when the skin blackens put the peppers into a plastic bag and leave them for 30 minutes. The skin will come off on its own.

Patetnik

Preparation time
15 minutes

Cooking time
10 minutes

Serves 4

Difficulty Easy

Ingredients

10 potatoes

1 onion, peeled and chopped

5 garlic cloves, peeled and chopped

200g goat cheese

100g cheese made from cow's milk

8 tablespoons oil

50g butter

4 sprigs of parsley, chopped

Preparation

Peel and wash the potatoes, dry well and grate them.

Mix together the grated potatoes, cheeses, onion, garlic, parsley, oil and butter.

Put them in a large pan and cook over a medium heat for 10 minutes, stirring all the time.

Serve hot.

Bulgaria

Potato fritters with feta

Preparation time
30 minutes

Cooking time
45 minutes

Serves 4

Difficulty Medium

Ingredients

750g potatoes

150g Bulgarian feta, crumbled

4 small spring onions, chopped

6 sprigs of dill, chopped

3 tablespoons olive oil

1 teaspoon lemon juice

4 tablespoons flour

1 egg

salt and pepper

Bulgaria

Preparation

Steam or boil the unpeeled potatoes for 25 minutes, peel and mash them.

Add the onions, dill, crumbled feta, lemon juice and egg. Season with salt and pepper and mix together thoroughly. Set aside in the fridge until the mixture is firm.

Form the mixture into small balls, flatten them slightly and roll them in the flour.

Heat the oil in a large pan and fry the fritters until golden brown on both sides. Drain on kitchen paper.

Serve hot.

Potato salad

Preparation time
10 minutes

Cooking time
25 minutes

Serves 4

Difficulty Easy

Ingredients

800g potatoes

3 onions, peeled and chopped

juice of half a lemon

6 tablespoons olive oil

4 sprigs of flat leaf parsley

salt and pepper

Preparation

Steam or boil the potatoes for 25 minutes, drain well and set aside to cool. When cool, peel and dice them into a large bowl.

In a small bowl mix together the lemon juice, olive oil and onions, season with salt and pepper. Pour the sauce over the potatoes and sprinkle with parsley.

Bulgaria

potato

How many species of potato are there?

The International Potato Center in Peru counts 7,500 species of potatoes (among which 1,950 are wild).

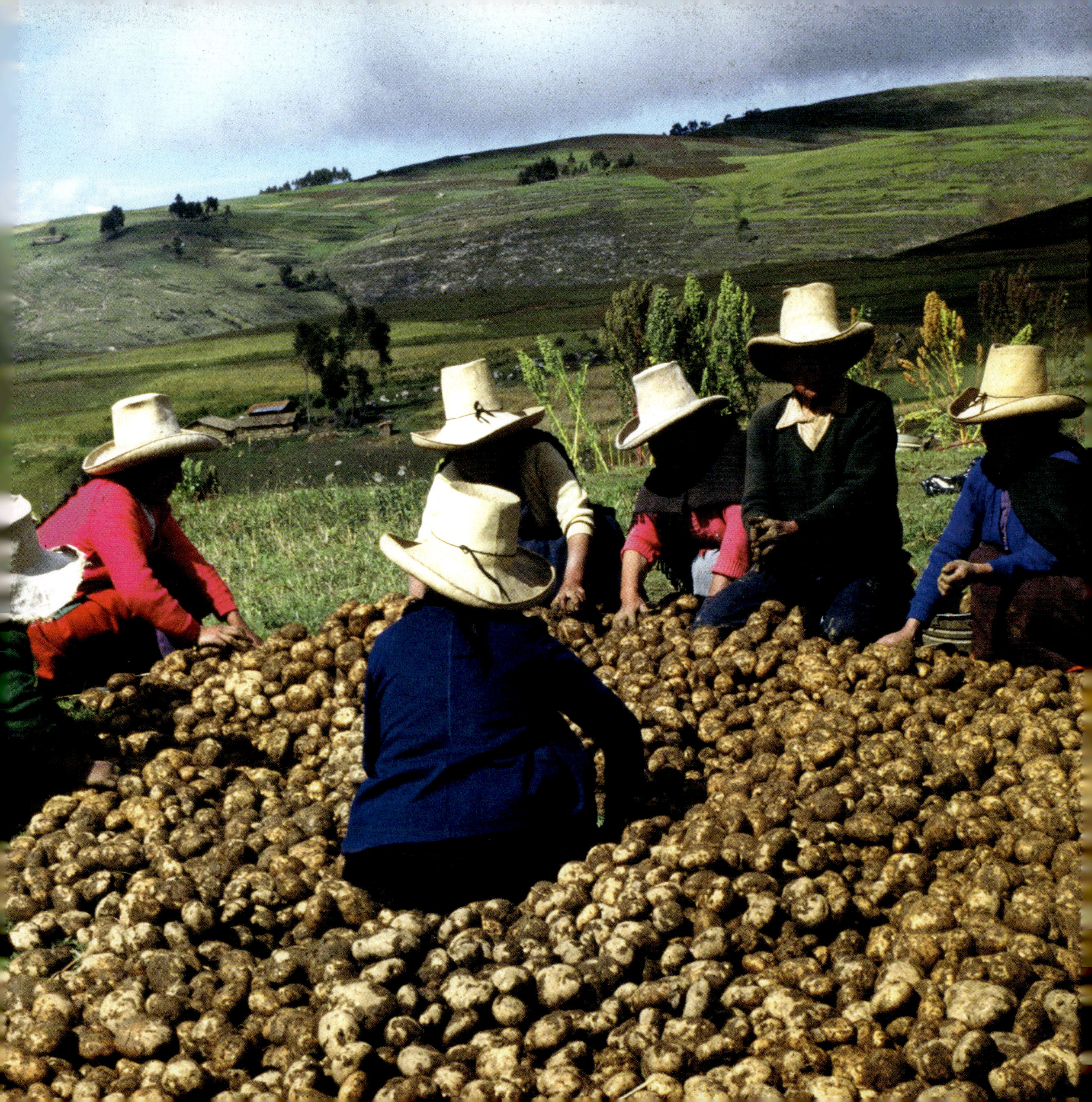

Potatoes with red beans

Preparation time
15 minutes

Cooking time
30 minutes

Serves 4

Difficulty Easy

Ingredients

4 medium-sized potatoes
1 tin red beans
100g cooked chicken breast
1 yellow onion, sliced into rings
1 red chilli
2 tablespoons peanut oil
salt and pepper

Cameroon

Preparation

Peel the potatoes, wash and dry them, and cut them into pieces. Wash and dry the chilli, discard the seeds and chop it finely.

Steam or cook the potatoes in boiling salted water for 20 minutes, then drain.

Heat the oil in a pan and brown the onion.

Chop the cooked chicken into small cubes.

Drain the red beans, combine with the potato and transfer to a serving dish. Arrange the chicken on top, garnish with the chilli and onion rings.

Serve hot.

Potato and salmon salad

Preparation time
20 minutes

Cooking time
25 minutes

Serves 4

Difficulty Easy

Ingredients

600g potatoes

400g fresh salmon

1 stick celery, washed, trimmed and finely chopped

1 spring onion, chopped

½ green pepper, diced

½ red pepper, diced

2 tablespoons maple cider vinegar

5 tablespoons vegetable oil

salt and pepper

a few dried cranberries, chopped

Preparation

Steam or boil the unpeeled potatoes for 25 minutes, peel them and slice into rounds.

Prepare the vinaigrette by combining the vinegar with the oil and a little salt and pepper. Pour it over the potatoes while they are still hot. Mix together and set aside to cool down at room temperature for several hours.

Poach the salmon in boiling salted water for 10 minutes, drain well and flake the flesh.

Add the salmon, peppers, onion and celery to the potatoes, and mix together carefully. Garnish with the dried cranberries.

Canada

Dried cranberries can be found in specialist grocery stores.

Potatoes with cheddar

Preparation time
10 minutes

Cooking time
15 minutes

Serves 4

Difficulty Easy

Ingredients

1 kg potatoes
1 tomato
2 shallots, peeled and finely chopped
1 tablespoon capers
4 slices of cheddar cheese
3 tablespoons olive oil
salt and pepper

Preparation

Steam or boil the potatoes for 20 minutes, then peel and cut them into rounds. Season with salt and pepper.

Peel the tomato, discard the seeds and chop into small pieces.

Heat the olive oil in a large pan and fry the potatoes on one side only until they are golden brown on the underside. Add the shallots, tomato and capers and continue cooking for 3 minutes. Then slide the whole mixture into a gratin dish.

Cover the potatoes with the slices of cheddar, then bake at 210°C for 10 minutes until the cheese is melted.

Serve hot.

Canada

Potato soup with dill

Preparation time
10 minutes

Cooking time
15 minutes

Serves 4

Difficulty Easy

Ingredients
500g potatoes
2 onions, peeled and chopped
300g tofu
1 litre chicken stock
1 tablespoon oil
4 sprigs of dill

Preparation

Peel the potatoes and chop them into small pieces.

In a large pan, fry the onion in the oil. Add the stock, potatoes and dill. Simmer for 20 minutes over a low heat.

Dice the tofu and stir it into the soup.

Serve hot.

Canada

Râpure

Preparation time
20 minutes

Cooking time
2 hours 30 minutes

Serves 4

Difficulty Easy

Ingredients

1 kg potatoes
1 kg loin of pork
2 onions, peeled and chopped
3 eggs
40g butter
salt and pepper

Preparation

Peel the potatoes, wash and dry them. Steam or cook half of them in boiling salted water for 25 minutes. Drain well and mash.

Cut the meat into small cubes. Melt the butter in a pan and cook the meat and onions for 15 minutes, stirring from time to time.

Grate the remaining potatoes and drain them well by squeezing out the moisture.

Preheat the oven to 180°C.

Combine the grated potato with the potatoes and meat mixture, season with salt and pepper. Transfer the mixture to a buttered oven dish. Bake in the oven for 2 hours and serve hot.

This is a typical Acadian dish of Nova Scotia.

Roasted cheese potatoes

Preparation time
15 minutes

Cooking time
1 hour 10 minutes

Serves 4

Difficulty Easy

Ingredients
4 large potatoes
100g butter
1 tablespoon fresh thyme
100g grated cheddar cheese
100g grated parmesan cheese
salt

Preparation

Peel the potatoes. Wash and dry them, cut each one into thin slices taking care not to cut entirely through the potato as you make the slices.

Arrange the potatoes in an oven dish.

Preheat the oven to 210°C.

Melt the butter and brush it over the potatoes. Add salt and a sprinkling of thyme. Bake in the oven for 50 minutes.

Remove the dish from the oven and sprinkle the grated cheddar and parmesan over the top. Put it back into the oven and cook for a further 10 minutes.

Serve hot.

Canada

This recipe comes from Prince Edward Island, a leading producer of potatoes.

Sweet potatoes with lemon butter

Preparation time
25 minutes

Cooking time
25 minutes

Serves 6

Difficulty Easy

Ingredients

1 kg sweet potatoes
50g butter
juice of 2 limes
100ml peanut oil
salt

Chad

Preparation

Peel the sweet potatoes and cut them into small chips.

Beat the lime juice into the butter, melt it in a pan and add the oil. When the mixture starts to bubble, add the sweet potatoes. Cook until golden brown. Drain on kitchen paper.

Sprinkle with salt and serve hot.

Charquican (vegetable and jerky stew)

Preparation time
10 minutes

Cooking time
40 minutes

Serves 4

Difficulty Easy

Ingredients

800g potatoes
250g courgettes, diced
600g beef, cubed
2 garlic cloves, peeled and finely chopped
2 onions, peeled and finely chopped
1 chilli, seeded and finely chopped
4 tablespoons oil
1tsp cumin
1 tablespoon dried oregano
salt and pepper

Preparation

Heat the oil in a frying pan and brown the meat with the onions and garlic. Add salt, pepper, cumin and oregano. Leave to cook for 10 minutes.

Peel the potatoes and cut them into small chunks.

Add the potatoes and courgettes to the pan, together with a glass of water. Cover and leave to cook on a low heat for about 30 minutes.

Add the chilli 5 minutes before the end of the cooking time.

Serve hot.

Chile

Charquican is Chile's national dish.

Chinese potato salad

Preparation time
20 minutes

Cooking time
15 minutes

Serves 4

Difficulty Easy

Ingredients

1 kg potatoes

8 green onions, peeled and chopped

5 grey shallots, peeled and chopped

2 small red chillies

4 stalks fresh mint, finely chopped

a medium bunch of fresh coriander, finely chopped

For the sauce:

60ml juice of a lime

1 egg yolk

1 teaspoon sesame oil

6 tablespoons hazelnut oil

2 teaspoons mirin sauce

4 sprigs fresh coriander

Preparation

Steam or boil the unpeeled potatoes for 25 minutes, drain and peel them. Cut them into quarters.

Wash and dry the chillies, discard the seeds and finely chop.

In a bowl combine the lime juice and egg yolk. Add the 2 oils drop by drop, whisking all the time, then add the mirin sauce.

Place the warm potatoes, chopped onion and shallots, chillies and coriander in a serving dish. Pour the sauce over the salad.

China

Ajiaco (chicken, corn and potato stew)

Preparation time
20 minutes

Cooking time
1 hour 10 minutes

Serves 4

Difficulty Easy

Ingredients

500g potatoes suitable for making soup
500g firm potatoes
2 onions, peeled and chopped
1 chicken, cut into pieces
1 litre chicken stock
bunch of fresh coriander
3 corn on the cob
bunch of guascas
2 avocados
1 red chilli
250ml cream
4 tablespoons capers
salt and pepper

Preparation

Put the chicken in a pan with the onions, coriander, salt and pepper. Cover with chicken stock and simmer for 15 minutes. Skim the surface from time to time.

Peel the soup potatoes, chop them into pieces and add to the pan. Leave to cook for 30 minutes.

Remove the chicken from the pan.

Peel the firm potatoes, chop them into pieces and add to the pan, with the guascas and corn. Continue cooking for 15 minutes.

Peel and cut the avocados into thin slices. Place in a small dish and sprinkle with lemon juice to prevent them from going black. Wash and dry the chilli, remove the seeds, chop finely and add to the avocado.

Mince the chicken flesh and return it to the pot to heat through.

Serve hot with the avocado and chilli, capers and cream.

Colombia

Guascas are aromatic plants found in Colombia. In this recipe you can replace them with cress.

Papas chorreadas (Potatoes with cream and tomato)

Preparation time
15 minutes

Cooking time
35 minutes

Serves 4

Difficulty Easy

Ingredients

1 kg potatoes
100g mozzarella, diced
30g butter
4 tomatoes, skinned, seeded and chopped
1 onion, peeled and finely chopped
100ml cream
4 sprigs of coriander
salt and pepper

Colombia

Preparation

Scrub the potatoes, steam or boil them for 25 minutes. Drain them and chop into cubes. Transfer them to a serving dish and set aside to keep warm.

Melt the butter in a frying pan, cook the onions and tomatoes for 5 minutes, then add the cream, mozzarella and chopped coriander leaves. Season with salt and pepper. When the cheese has melted, pour the sauce over the potatoes.

Serve hot.

Papas en azucar

Preparation time
20 minutes

Cooking time
35 minutes

Serves 4

Difficulty Easy

Ingredients

600g potatoes, peeled
200g icing sugar
200g flour
juice of 1 lemon
oil for deep frying

Preparation

Peel the potatoes, steam or boil them for 25 minutes, then mash them.

Add the lemon juice, sugar and flour. Knead to obtain a smooth dough.

Roll the dough out on a lightly floured surface. Using a cutter, cut out patties.

Heat the frying oil and deep fry the patties for a few minutes until golden brown.

Serve hot.

If you don't have a cutter, turn a glass upside down and use that.

Colombia

Sweet potato stew

Preparation time
15 minutes

Cooking time
2 hours 30 minutes

Serves 4

Difficulty Easy

Ingredients

6 sweet potatoes
600g beef, diced
6 tablespoons tomato concentrate
2 onions, peeled and chopped
1 chilli, seeded and finely chopped
6 tablespoons palm oil
4 pinches of ground nutmeg
salt and pepper

Congo

Preparation

Heat the oil in a frying pan, add the meat, chilli, onions, tomato concentrate and a glass of water. Season with salt, pepper and the nutmeg. Cover and leave to simmer for 2 hours.

Peel the sweet potatoes and cut them into chunks. Add them to the pan and cook for another 30 minutes.

Serve hot.

Potatoes are usually grown by planting a tuber piece on which two or three eyes have formed. Each plant can produce from 2 to 10 new tubers.

Chayote

Preparation time
20 minutes

Cooking time
45 minutes

Serves 4

Difficulty Easy

Ingredients
4 potatoes
2 small aubergines, sliced
200g green beans
1 carrot, peeled and thinly sliced
5 tomatoes, skinned, seeded and diced
8 lamb chops
3 garlic cloves, peeled and chopped
1 sprig of oregano
1 sprig of thyme
120ml oil
2 sprigs of fresh rosemary
1 teaspoon paprika
salt and pepper

Preparation

Steam or boil the unpeeled potatoes for 25 minutes, peel and slice them.

Place the sliced aubergines in a colander, sprinkle them with salt and leave to drain for 20 minutes. Rinse and dry them on kitchen paper.

Cook the beans in boiling salted water for about 10 minutes, then drain them.

Heat 100ml of the oil in a frying pan. Add the garlic, aubergines, tomatoes, green beans, carrots and potatoes. Season with salt and pepper, add the oregano and thyme. Fry for 10 minutes, stirring all the time. Lower the heat and continue cooking gently.

With the rest of the oil fry the lamb chops in a separate pan for 10 minutes, with the rosemary and paprika, turning them over halfway through.

Transfer the vegetables to a serving dish and arrange the lamp chops on top.

Costa Rica

Potato balls with spinach

Côte d'Ivoire

Preparation time
20 minutes

Cooking time
40 minutes

Serves 4

Difficulty Medium

Ingredients

500g potatoes
175g fresh spinach, trimmed and washed
125g flour
2 shallots, peeled and chopped
1 garlic clove, peeled and chopped
2 tablespoons olive oil
300ml tomato sauce
2 teaspoons brown sugar
salt

Preparation

Peel the potatoes, steam or cook them for 25 minutes in boiling salted water. Drain well and mash.

Blanch the spinach in boiling water for 2 minutes. Drain out as much water as possible, and chop.

Place the mash onto a lightly floured surface. In the centre put the spinach, a pinch of salt, a teaspoon of olive oil and 2 tablespoons of flour. Combine well, then mix in the rest of the flour to obtain a thick dough.

Form the dough into balls.

Poach the balls in boiling salted water for 5 minutes. As soon as they rise to the surface, remove with a slotted spoon and drain on kitchen paper.

In a pan combine the garlic, shallots, the rest of the oil, tomato sauce and sugar. Cook for 10 minutes. Pour over the potato balls.

Sweet potato gratin

Preparation time
20 minutes

Cooking time
50 minutes

Serves 4

Difficulty Easy

Ingredients

1 kg sweet potatoes
750ml milk
3 garlic cloves, peeled and chopped
3 eggs, beaten
100g grated cheese
2 pinches of grated nutmeg
2 pinches of ground ginger
30g butter
salt and pepper

Preparation

Peel the sweet potatoes and chop them finely. Place the garlic and the potatoes in a large pan, add salt, pepper, the nutmeg and ginger, cover with the milk and cook over a low heat for 30 minutes.

Butter a gratin dish. Remove the potatoes with a slotted spoon and arrange them in the dish.

Bring the milk to the boil and cook it over a high heat until reduced by about half.

Preheat the oven to 210°C.

Add the milk to the beaten eggs, then pour over the sweet potatoes.

Sprinkle with grated cheese and bake in the oven for 20 minutes.

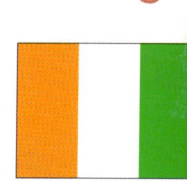

Serve hot.

Côte d'Ivoire

Burek with potatoes

Preparation time
25 minutes

Cooking time
35 minutes

Serves 4

Difficulty Easy

Ingredients

4 potatoes
1 onion, peeled and finely chopped
4 sheets of brick dough or filo pastry
300g minced meat
50g butter
4 tablespoons oil
salt and pepper

Croatia

Preparation

Peel and wash the potatoes, dry and dice them.

Mix together the potatoes, onion and minced meat. Season with salt and pepper.

Preheat the oven to 180°C.

Spread a sheet of filo pastry on a lightly floured work surface and brush it with a little oil. Spread some of the mixture over it and roll it up. Do the same with the other sheets. Arrange them in a gratin dish.

Melt the butter and pour it over the dish. Bake in the oven for 30 minutes.

Potatoes are ready to be harvested when the leaves of the plant start yellowing and dying.

Sweet potato cake

Preparation time
15 minutes

Cooking time
1 hour 5 minutes

Serves 6

Difficulty Easy

Ingredients

1 kg sweet potatoes
500ml milk
1 vanilla pod
4 eggs
100g sugar
1 sachet of vanilla-flavoured sugar
150g butter
200ml rum
redcurrant jelly

Preparation

Peel the sweet potatoes. Bring the milk to the boil, add the vanilla bean and cook the potatoes for 20 minutes. Drain and mash them.

Melt the butter. Beat the eggs in a mixing bowl and add the butter, sugar, vanilla-flavoured sugar and rum. Stir in the mashed sweet potatoes.

Preheat the oven to 150°C.

Transfer the potatoes to a buttered cake tin and bake in the oven for 45 minutes.

Leave to cool, turn the cake out and top with melted redcurrant jelly.

Cuba

Kleftiko

Preparation time
10 minutes

Cooking time
3 hours

Serves 4

Difficulty Easy

Ingredients

1 kg potatoes
600g tomatoes, sliced
1 kg shoulder of lamb
3 bay leaves, chopped
juice of 1 lemon
bunch of flat leaf parsley
salt and pepper

Cyprus

Preparation

Peel the potatoes, wash and slice them into rounds.

Cut the lamb into medium-sized pieces.

Put all the ingredients into a large bowl, season with salt and pepper, and mix together.

Preheat the oven to 150°C.

Transfer to a baking pot and cover it tightly – it is important that the pot be sealed. Bake in the oven for 3 hours.

To seal the pot, use a paste made by mixing 5 tablespoons of flour with 2 tablespoons of water.

Bohemian potato soup

Preparation time
15 minutes

Cooking time
30 minutes

Serves 4

Difficulty Easy

Ingredients

300g potatoes
1 onion, peeled and finely chopped
200g white mushrooms
4 eggs
500ml crème fraîche
1 litre vegetable stock
1 tablespoon caraway seeds
1 bay leaf
4 sprigs of dill, chopped
1 tablespoon vinegar
salt and pepper

Preparation

Peel and dice the potatoes.

Put the vegetable stock in a large pan, add the onion, bay leaf, caraway seeds and potatoes. Season with salt and pepper and cook for 15 minutes.

Wash and dry the mushrooms, add them to the pan together with the vinegar and cook for another 10 minutes.

Mix the flour with the crème fraîche, transfer to the pan stirring all the time, and bring to the boil, still stirring.

Break the eggs one at a time into a ladle and slide each one gently into the soup to poach. Cook for a further 3 minutes.

Remove the eggs carefully with a slotted spoon. Prepare 4 soup bowls and place an egg in each. Fill the bowls with soup and garnish with dill. Serve hot.

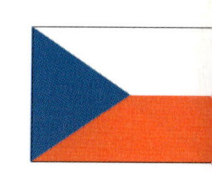

Czech Republic

Potato gratin

Preparation time
20 minutes

Cooking time
1 hour

Serves 4

Difficulty Easy

Ingredients

1 kg potatoes
6 hard-boiled eggs, sliced
30g butter
250g crème fraîche
200g grated cheese
4 tablespoons paprika
salt and pepper

Czech Republic

Preparation

Steam or boil the unpeeled potatoes for about 25 minutes. Drain and peel them and cut them into slices.

Preheat the oven to 180°C. Butter an oven dish.

In the oven dish, arrange a layer of potato, a little salt, pepper and paprika, a little cream, a layer of sliced egg. Continue in layers, ending with potatoes. Pour the rest of the cream over the top and sprinkle with cheese.

Bake in the oven for 15 minutes.

Serve hot.

Potato quenelles

Preparation time
25 minutes

Cooking time
40 minutes

Serves 4

Difficulty Medium

Ingredients

500g potatoes
1 onion, peeled and chopped
1 egg, beaten
75g butter
125g flour
salt

Preparation

Peel the potatoes, cut them into quarters, steam or cook them in boiling salted water for 20 minutes.

Fry the onion in a knob of butter.

Drain and mash the potatoes. Add the onion, flour, beaten egg, a little salt and the rest of the butter. Combine well to form a smooth dough.

Form quenelles with the dough. Bring a pan of salted water to the boil, lower the heat and poach the quenelles for 15 minutes. Remove them with a slotted spoon and drain on kitchen paper.

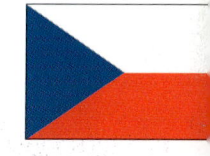

Serve hot.

Czech Republic

Serve as an accompaniment to roast meat.

potato

Who discovered the potato?

When the Spanish conquistador Fransisco Pizarro set foot on the Peruvian coast in 1524, he found that the Incas had been growing and harvesting potatoes for centuries. Together with the corncob and the bean, it sustained them all year round.

A long time ago, in order to preserve the nutritional values of potatoes, the Andean Indians had already resorted to a technique that, rudimentary though it was, was nonetheless effective in preserving nutritional values. The part of the harvest that had to be preserved for at least a year was exposed to frost at night. This brief freezing had the effect of softening the tubers. Women and children then trampled them with their bare feet in the same way our ancestors did with the grapes for winemaking.

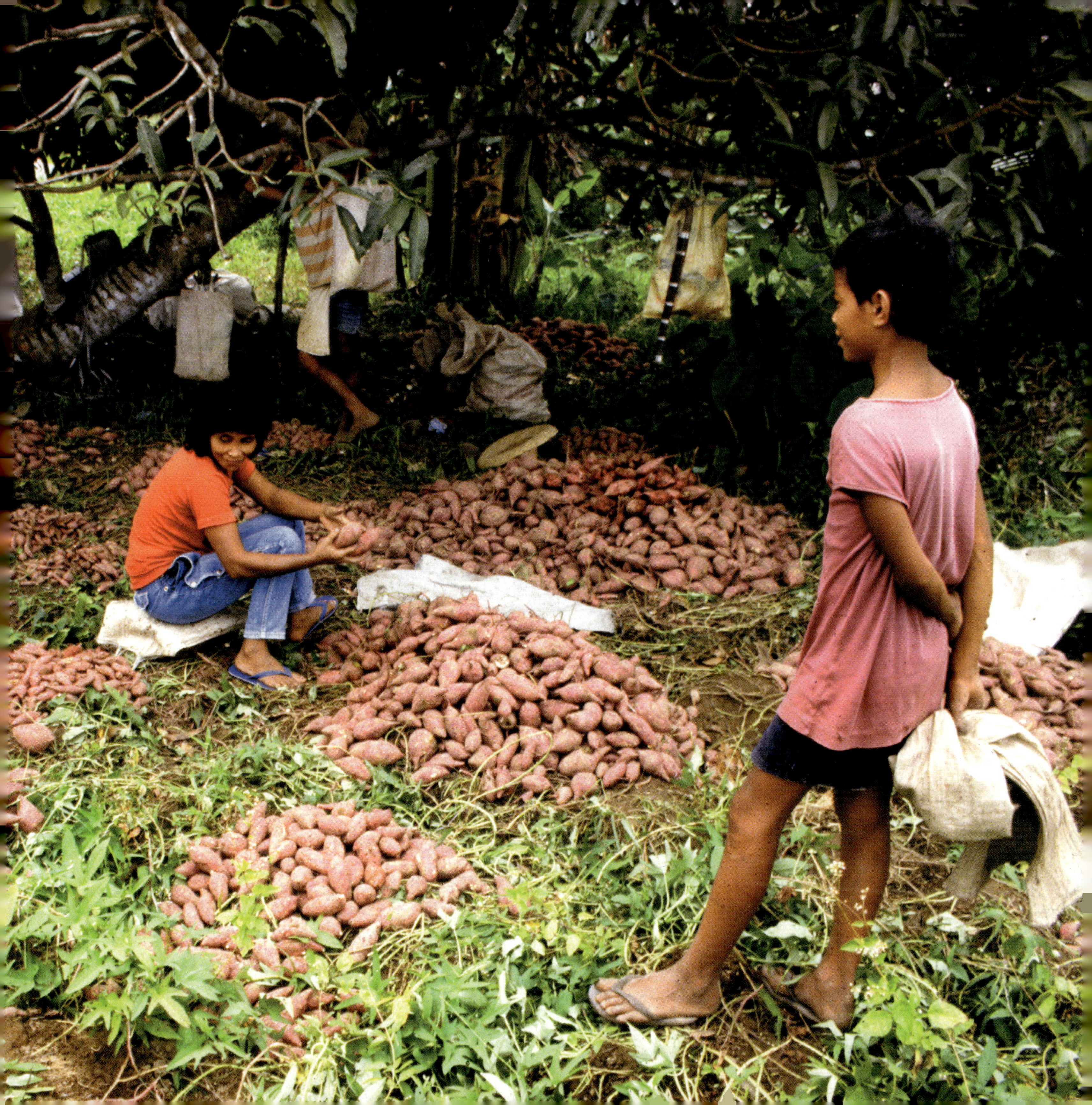

Brændende kærlighed

Preparation time
15 minutes

Cooking time
40 minutes

Serves 4

Difficulty Easy

Ingredients

1 kg potatoes
300g smoked bacon
3 onions, peeled and finely chopped
200ml milk
50g butter
salt and pepper

Preparation

Peel the potatoes, steam or boil them for 25 minutes.

Dry fry (without oil or fat) the slices of bacon in a pan. Remove them from the pan, keeping the bacon fat, and set aside, keeping them warm.

Fry the onions in the bacon fat.

Drain the potatoes, mash them and add the milk, butter, salt and pepper. Transfer to a serving dish, scoop out a hollow in the middle and put the onions and the bacon in it.

Serve hot.

This very common Danish family dish can also be prepared with mashed split peas and smoked pork shoulder.

Denmark

Caramel potatoes

Preparation time
15 minutes

Cooking time
35 minutes

Serves 4

Difficulty Easy

Ingredients
1 kg potatoes
100g butter
100g castor sugar
salt

Preparation

Steam or boil the unpeeled potatoes in salted water for 20 minutes. Drain and set aside. Peel them when they are cool.

Place the sugar in a non-stick pan, add a tablespoon of water. Cook over high heat until golden brown, then add the butter a little at a time, stirring all the time.

When the butter is melted, add the potatoes, rolling them around so they are completely coated with caramel. Cook for another 5 minutes.

Serve hot.

Denmark

Pick potatoes which are all the same size – small and round.

Curried potato salad

Preparation time
20 minutes

Cooking time
25 minutes

Serves 4

Difficulty Easy

Ingredients

800g potatoes
150g peas
1 onion, peeled and chopped
2 tablespoons chopped chives
100g mayonnaise
2 plain yoghurts
2 tablespoons vinegar
1 tablespoon mustard
1 teaspoon curry powder
salt and pepper

Denmark

Preparation

Steam or boil the unpeeled potatoes for 20-25 minutes, depending on their size. Set aside to cool completely, then peel and slice them.

Add the onion and peas to the potatoes and mix together.

In a large bowl whip together the mayonnaise, curry powder, yoghurt and vinegar, season with salt and pepper.

Pour the sauce over the potatoes, mix together and set aside for an hour before serving.

West Indian mash

Preparation time
15 minutes

Cooking time
15 minutes

Serves 4

Difficulty Easy

Ingredients

800g potatoes
2 bananas, peeled and sliced
1 egg, beaten
100g cream
50g butter
4 cm piece of root ginger
2 small chillies
2 drops liquid vanilla

Preparation

Peel the potatoes and chop into pieces. Wash the chillies, discard the seeds and cut them into slices.

Put the potatoes, bananas, ginger and chillies in a pan of water flavoured with the vanilla and cook for 15 minutes. Drain, keeping the cooking liquid, and mash the mixture.

Add the butter, cream and egg to the mash. If it is too thick add a few spoonfuls of the cooking liquid.

Serve hot.

Dominica

It is not unusual for Peruvian farmers to cultivate up to 40 varieties of potato. This is a wise precaution aimed at preserving those plants which are less sensitive than others to disease, frost, drought, hail, etc.

Stewed turkey with potatoes

Preparation time
20 minutes

Cooking time
2 hours

Serves 4

Difficulty Easy

Ingredients
8 small potatoes
800g skinless pieces of turkey
1 green pepper, seeded and cut into fine strips
1 red pepper, seeded and cut into fine strips
250g peas
2 onions, peeled and chopped
4 garlic cloves, peeled and chopped
4 tablespoons flour
2 tablespoons vegetable oil
750ml chicken stock
4 tablespoons tomato purée
12 green olives, with stones removed
6 tablespoons capers
salt and pepper

Preparation

Peel the potatoes and cut them into quarters.

Roll the turkey pieces in the flour. Heat the oil in a pan that can also go in the oven. Fry the turkey for 10 minutes, turning often, until golden brown on all sides. Add the garlic, onion and peppers and cook for 10 minutes stirring all the time.

Preheat the oven to 180°C.

Add the tomato purée and chicken stock, bring to the boil. Cover and put in the oven.

Cook for 1 hour, then add the olives, capers and potatoes. Put the dish back in the oven and cook for 30 minutes. Finally, add the peas and cook for a further 10 minutes. Add salt and pepper.

Serve hot.

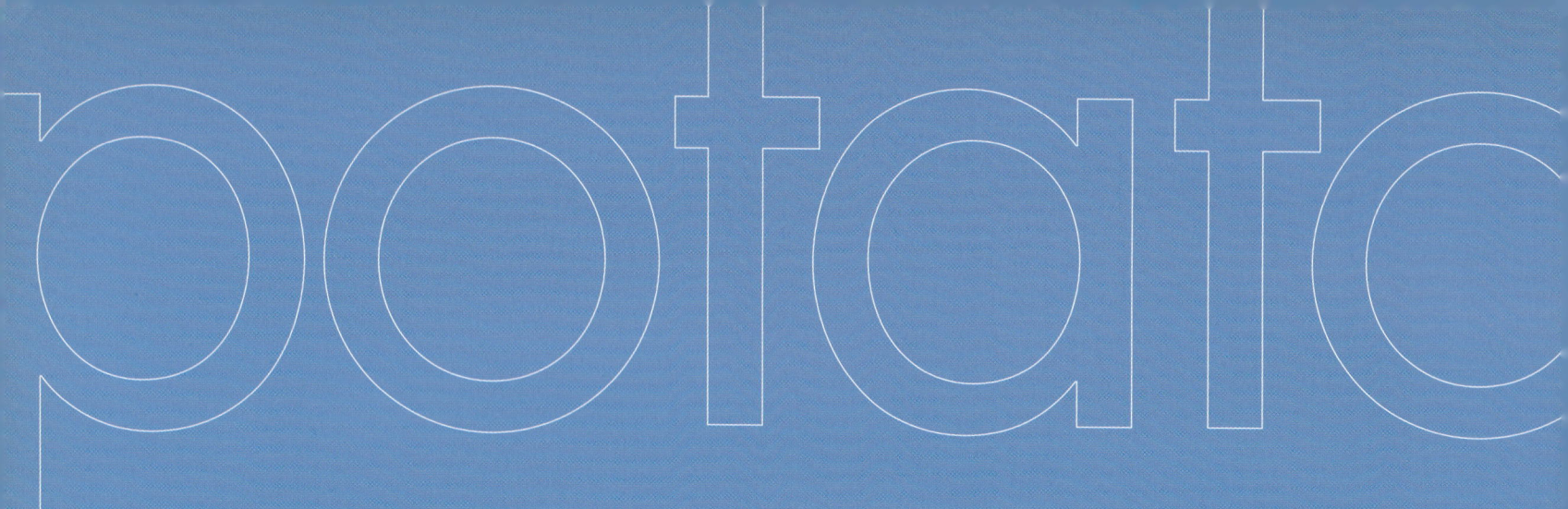

How much vitamin C does a potato contain?

The quantity of vitamin C in a medium-sized potato is quite considerable: 25mg per 100g, which is about one half of the daily requirement of vitamin C. Other staples such as rice and wheat have none.

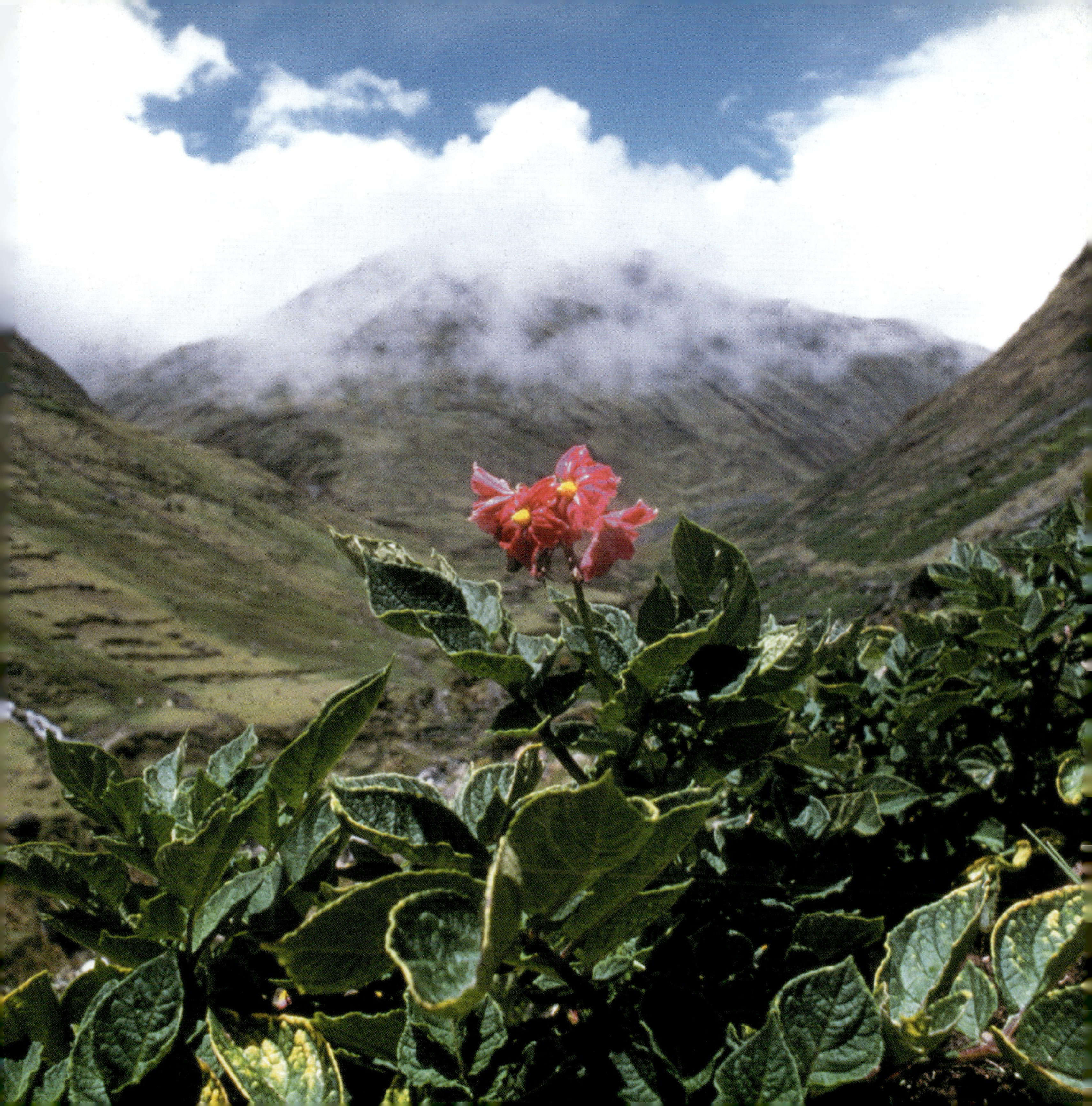

Lettuce and potato salad

Preparation time
20 minutes

Cooking time
40 minutes

Serves 4 to 6

Difficulty Easy

Ingredients
4 potatoes
½ lettuce
250g green beans
150g peas
1 tomato
1 hard-boiled egg, sliced

For the dressing:
2 tablespoons lemon juice
2 tablespoons olive oil
2 tablespoons chicken stock
1 teaspoon mustard
salt and pepper

Preparation

Cut the beans into short lengths and cook in boiling salted water for 10 minutes. Set aside to cool.

Steam or boil the unpeeled potatoes for 25 minutes. Let them cool down, then peel and dice them.

Cook the peas in boiling water for 10 minutes, drain and set aside to cool.

Skin, seed and chop the tomato. Wash the lettuce and slice it into thin strips.

Place the lettuce and the vegetables in a salad bowl.

In a mixing bowl whisk together the chicken stock, mustard, lemon juice, oil, and a little salt and pepper. Pour the dressing over the salad and mix carefully.

Garnish with the slices of egg and serve cold.

Ecuador

Khoudare belhalba

Preparation time
10 minutes

Cooking time
30 minutes

Serves 4

Difficulty Easy

Ingredients

500g potatoes

500g aubergines, washed and diced

2 onions, peeled and chopped

juice of 1 lemon

1 teaspoon fennel seeds

1 teaspoon fenugreek seeds

50g butter

100ml water

salt

Preparation

Peel and wash the potatoes, dry and dice them.

Melt the butter in a frying pan, add the fennel and fenugreek seeds, the vegetables and lemon juice. Season with salt and add the water. Cover and leave to simmer for 30 minutes.

Serve hot or warm.

Egypt

Fenugreek is an aromatic plant whose seeds when ground are used in cooking and baking.

Tagane batatesse

Preparation time
20 minutes

Cooking time
50 minutes

Serves 4

Difficulty Easy

Ingredients

1 kg potatoes

500g shoulder of lamb, diced

1 garlic clove, peeled and chopped

2 bay leaves

2 tablespoons thyme

2 sprigs of parsley, chopped

50g butter

2 pinches of cinnamon

salt and pepper

Preparation

Peel and wash the potatoes, dry and slice them.

Preheat the oven to 180°C.

In a mixing bowl combine the garlic, parsley, bay leaves, thyme, cinnamon, salt and pepper.

Grease an oven dish. Arrange in it a layer of potatoes, then diced meat and herb mixture. Continue until all the ingredients have been used. Dot with knobs of butter and bake in the oven for 50 minutes.

Serve hot.

Egypt

Meat stuffed potato pancakes

Preparation time
30 minutes

Cooking time
50 minutes

Serves 4

Difficulty Medium

Ingredients

800g potatoes
800g minced pork or beef
1 onion, peeled and chopped
2 eggs
2 tablespoons flour
8 tablespoons oil
salt and pepper
sour cream

Preparation

In a bowl combine the meat, onion, salt and pepper.

Steam or boil the unpeeled potatoes for 25 minutes. Peel and mash them. Add the eggs, flour, salt and pepper and mix together thoroughly.

Form pancakes with the potato purée. In the centre of each put a spoonful of meat and close the pancake over it so that the meat is sealed inside.

Heat the oil in a large frying pan. Fry the pancakes over a medium heat for 10 minutes until golden brown on both sides. Drain on kitchen paper.

Serve hot with sour cream.

Estonia

Andean farmers can cultivate up to 3,000 varieties of potato.

Rosolje

Preparation time
30 minutes

Cooking time
35 minutes

Serves 4 to 6

Difficulty Easy

Ingredients

600g potatoes
4 smoked herring fillets
3 cooked beetroots
2 onions, peeled and chopped
2 hard-boiled eggs, sliced
200g ham, chopped
1 tablespoon whole grain mustard
2 tablespoons cider vinegar
½ teaspoon sugar
350ml sour cream
1 teaspoon horseradish
4 sprigs of dill, chopped
salt and pepper

Preparation

The day before, soak the herring fillets in cold water for 12 hours to remove the salt.

On the day, drain and dry the herring on kitchen paper and cut into fine strips.

Steam or boil the unpeeled potatoes for 25 minutes. Drain, peel and cut them into cubes. Skin the beetroots and cut them into cubes the same size.

Place the potatoes, beetroots, eggs, onion, ham and herring in a serving bowl.

In a separate bowl combine the mustard, vinegar, sugar, cream, horseradish, salt and pepper. Pour over the salad. Garnish with dill.

Estonia

Sweet potato and garlic soufflé

Preparation time
30 minutes

Cooking time
35 minutes

Serves 4

Difficulty Easy

Ingredients
750g sweet potatoes
8 garlic cloves, crushed
75g butter
1 egg, beaten
60g cream
4 tablespoons breadcrumbs
4 pinches of nutmeg

Preparation

Peel the sweet potatoes and cook in boiling water for 25 minutes. Drain and slice them.

Preheat the oven to 210°C.

In a bowl mix together the garlic, beaten egg, cream and nutmeg.

Arrange the potato slices in a gratin dish, add the garlic sauce, sprinkle with the breadcrumbs and finally drizzle with melted butter.

Bake in the oven for 10 minutes so that the top is golden brown.

Serve hot.

Ethiopia

potato

How many potatoes are grown in the world?

Nowadays, the potato is the fourth most important food crop in the world, with an annual production approaching 300 million tons.

More than one third of the global potato output now comes from developing countries, up from 11 per cent in the early 1960s.

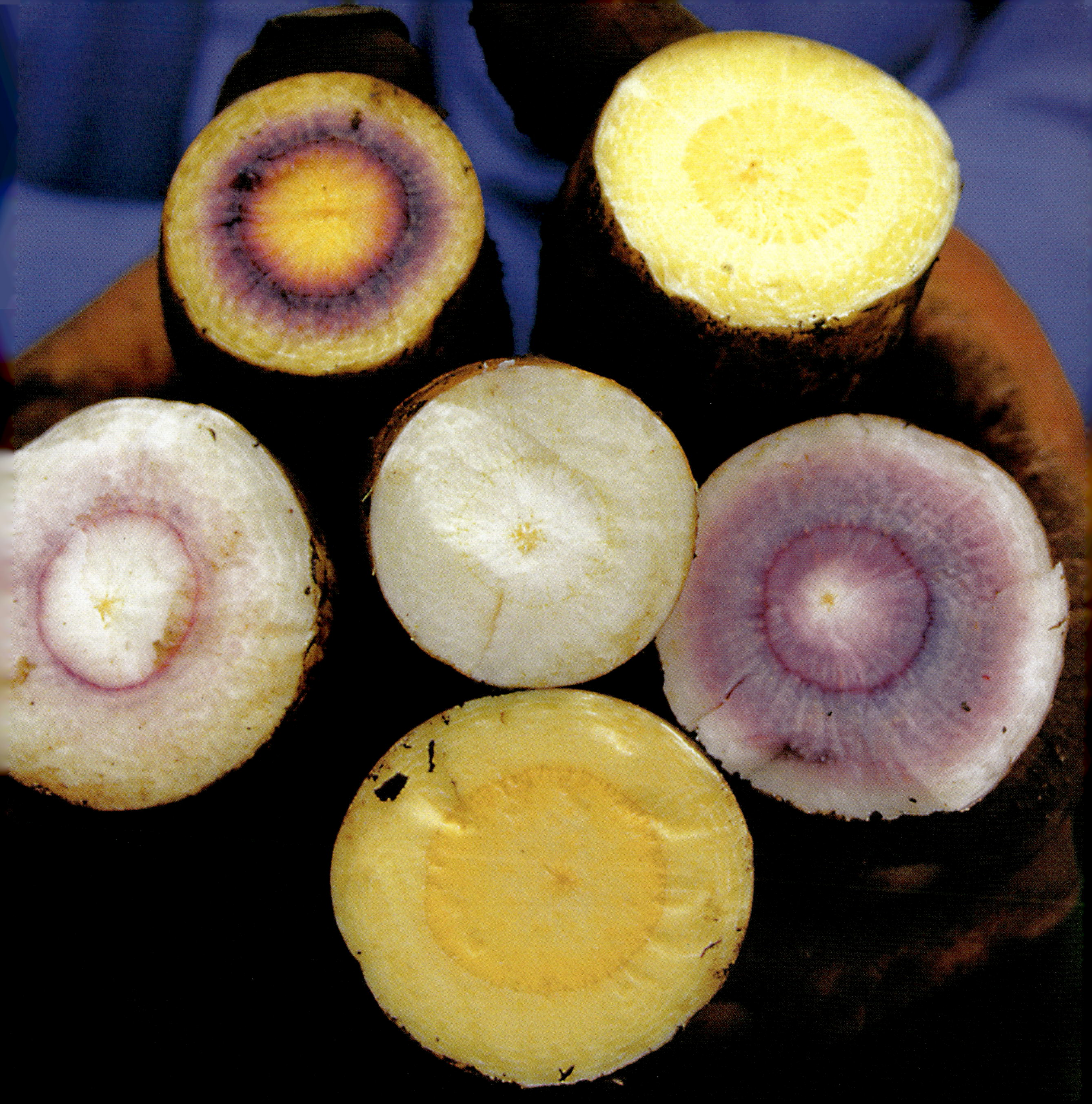

Potato and herring casserole

Preparation time
20 minutes

Cooking time
1 hour 5 minutes

Serves 4 to 6

Difficulty Easy

Ingredients

2 large salted herrings
500g potatoes
4 small spring onions, chopped
2 eggs
500ml milk
40g butter
2 tablespoons breadcrumbs

Finland

Preparation

Soak the herrings in a dish filled with water for 6 hours. Drain, remove the skin and bones, and chop up the flesh.

Steam or boil the unpeeled potatoes for 25 minutes, peel and cut into slices.

Preheat the oven to 180°C.

Butter an ovenproof dish. Melt the rest of the butter in the dish.

Place a layer of potato slices in the dish, then a layer of herring and some onion. Continue in layers, ending with a layer of potatoes. Pour the melted butter over the top.

Beat the eggs with the milk, season with pepper. Pour over the dish and sprinkle with breadcrumbs. Bake in the oven for 40 minutes.

Serve hot.

Aligot

Preparation time
15 minutes

Cooking time
40 minutes

Serves 6

Difficulty Easy

Ingredients

600g potatoes
400g ripe Tomme de Laguiole (Cantal)
1 clove garlic, crushed
150ml cream
60g butter
salt and pepper

Preparation

Steam or boil the unpeeled potatoes for about 25 minutes.

Cut the cheese into strips.

Drain the potatoes, peel and mash them. Transfer them to a large pan, add the garlic, butter and cream. Season with salt and pepper and mix together.

Heat the mash over a gentle heat. As soon as it is very hot, stir in the cheese. Serve as soon as the cheese is melted.

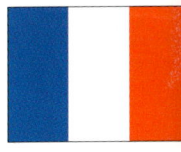

France

This is a traditional dish of the Massif Central region.

Bibeleskaes

Preparation time
20 minutes

Cooking time
1 hour

Serves 4

Difficulty Easy

Ingredients

8 large potatoes
1 kg fromage blanc
4 small spring onions, peeled and chopped
2 garlic cloves, peeled and chopped
1 shallot, peeled and chopped
1 bunch of chives, chopped
salt and pepper

France

Preparation

Scrub the potatoes and put them in an oven dish. Brush them with a little oil, sprinkle with coarse salt and cook in the oven at 210°C for 1 hour.

Put the fromage blanc in a serving dish and season with salt and pepper.

Put the onions, garlic, shallot and chives in 4 separate little dishes.

Serve the potatoes hot with the separate dishes.

This is a typical Alsace dish.

Gratin dauphinois

Preparation time
20 minutes

Cooking time
60 minutes

Serves 4

Difficulty Easy

Ingredients

1 kg potatoes
200ml milk
2 garlic cloves
200ml cream
150g grated gruyère cheese
100g butter
salt, pepper and nutmeg

Preparation

Peel and rinse the potatoes, dry them and cut into thin slices. Transfer them to a bowl.

Crush the garlic over the potatoes, add the milk, season with salt and pepper and a little nutmeg and combine together.

Preheat the oven to 180°C.

Butter a gratin dish, transfer the potatoes, spread the cream over the top and sprinkle with the grated gruyère.

Bake in the over for 60 minutes.

Serve hot.

France

Potato matelote

Preparation time
10 minutes

Cooking time
30 minutes

Serves 4

Difficulty Easy

Ingredients

1 kg potatoes
2 onions, peeled and finely chopped
500ml beef stock
100ml red wine
1 tablespoon flour
50g butter
1 bouquet garni
pepper

France

Preparation

Peel the potatoes and cut into slices.

Melt the butter in a pan and brown the onions. Sprinkle with flour, then add the red wine and stock. Add the bouquet garni and pepper, and then the potatoes. Mix together.

Cover and leave to simmer for 30 minutes.

Serve hot.

Pâté bourbonnais

Preparation time
20 minutes

Cooking time
1 hour 30 minutes

Serves 4

Difficulty Easy

Ingredients

1 kg potatoes

1 onion, peeled and finely chopped

2 circles ready-made shortcrust pastry

500ml cream

30g butter

1 egg yolk

3 tablespoons milk

6 sprigs flat leaf parsley, chopped

salt, pepper and nutmeg

Preparation

Butter a tart ring generously and line it with half the pastry.

Peel and rinse the potatoes, dry and cut into slices ½ cm thick. Place in a large bowl. Add the onion, parsley, season with salt, pepper and a little nutmeg, and mix together.

Pour the potatoes into the tart ring. Cover with the other circle of pastry and press the edges together firmly.

Make a hole in the middle of the pastry lid and keep it open by using a small piece of cardboard so that the steam can escape (or use a pastry chimney).

Preheat the oven to 180°C.

Beat the egg yolk with the milk and brush it over the pastry.

Bake in the oven for 1 – 1½ hours, until cooked. Use the tip of a sharp knife to test when the potatoes are cooked.

Pour the cream through the hole in the top of the pastry and serve immediately.

France

To seal the edges of the pastry, pinch them with wet fingers.

Sarladais potatoes

Preparation time
15 minutes

Cooking time
30 minutes

Serves 4

Difficulty Easy

Ingredients

800g potatoes
2 garlic cloves, crushed
3 tablespoons goose grease
4 sprigs parsley, chopped
salt and pepper

France

Preparation

Peel and rinse the potatoes and cut them into slices about ½ cm thick.

Melt the goose grease in a frying pan over a low heat, add the potatoes and fry them for 15 minutes, stirring often.

Combine the garlic and parsley. Add to the potatoes, season with salt and pepper and continue cooking for 15 minutes, stirring often.

Serve hot.

This dish, named after the town of Sarlat, in the Périgord, is one of the finest in French gastronomy.

Soufflé potatoes

Preparation time
25 minutes

Cooking time
15 minutes

Serves 4

Difficulty Easy

Ingredients
1 kg potatoes
2 litres olive oil
salt

Preparation

Peel and rinse the potatoes, dry and cut into thick slices.

Put the oil in a fryer and heat to 150°C. Plunge the potato slices into the oil and leave them to cook for 8 minutes, stirring all the time. Lift out of the oil and drain.

Heat the oil to 220°C and put the potatoes back into the fryer. Leave to cook for 3 minutes, stirring them so that they can swell.

Remove from the oil and dry on kitchen paper. Season with salt just before serving.

France

On 26 August 1837, a cook was awaiting the arrival of King Louis-Philippe and Queen Marie-Amélie. Since they were late, the cook had to remove his potatoes from the oil to prevent them from burning. When he plunged them back into the very hot oil he was surprised to see them puff up like little balloons. The King congratulated him on his recipe and the dish became very popular.

Vichyssoise

Preparation time
15 minutes

Cooking time
35 minutes

Serves 4

Difficulty Easy

Ingredients

500g potatoes

3 leeks, white part only, sliced into fine strips

2 onions, peeled and chopped

1 litre chicken stock

500ml cream

30g butter

small bunch of chives, snipped

salt and pepper

France

Preparation

Melt the butter in a pan. Add the leek and onion and cook on a low heat until softened.

Peel and rinse the potatoes, dry and cut into cubes. Add them to the pan, add the stock and bring to the boil. Lower the heat and simmer for 20 minutes.

Liquidise the soup, stir in the cream and leave to cool at room temperature, then chill for 2 hours.

Sprinkle with chives just before serving.

Vichyssoise was created at the New York Ritz Carlton hotel at the beginning of the last century by a chef from the Bourbonnais.

Zembrocal

Preparation time
15 minutes

Cooking time
30 minutes

Serves 4

Difficulty Easy

Ingredients

2 large potatoes

500g rice

2 onions, peeled and chopped

3 garlic cloves, peeled and chopped

4 tablespoons oil

1 tablespoon fresh thyme chopped

½ teaspoon curcuma

salt

Preparation

Peel the potatoes and cut into small chunks.

Heat the oil in a large pan and fry the potato. Add a glass of water and bring to the oil, then lower the heat and allow to simmer.

Combine the onion, garlic, thyme, curcuma and a little salt. Add the mixture to the potatoes.

Rinse the rice several times. In a pan, cover the rice with water and add the potatoes. Bring to the boil, then lower the heat, half cover the pan and simmer over a gentle heat for 20 minutes.

Serve hot.

France

potato

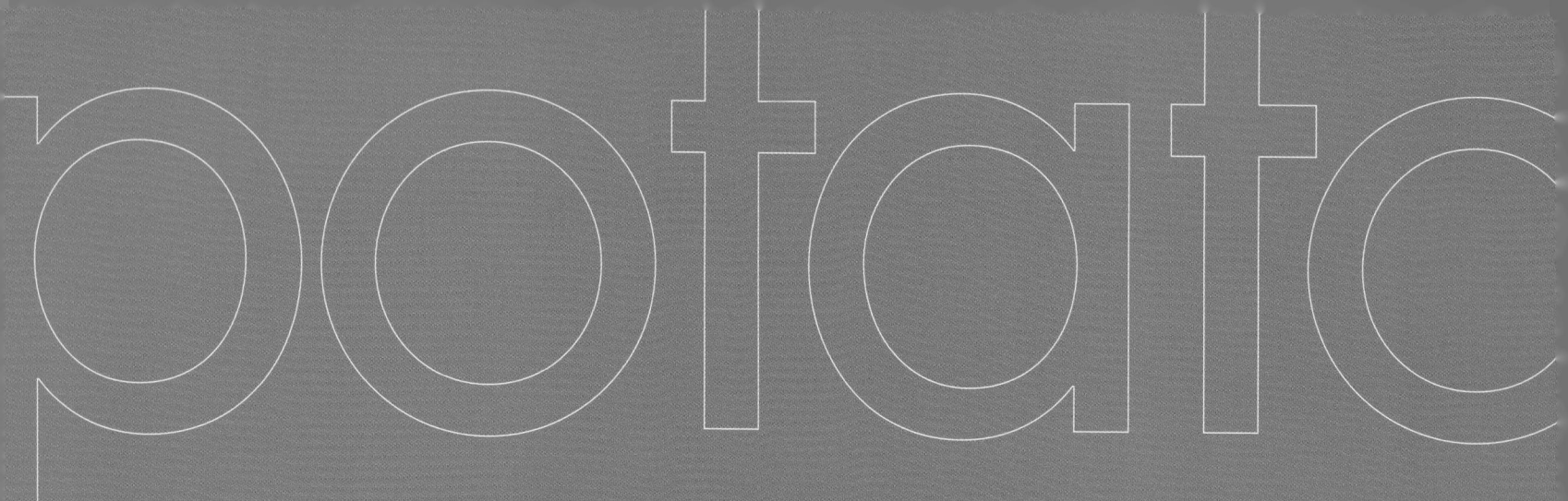

Which disease is considered to be the most serious for potatoes?

Late blight is considered to be the most serious potato disease worldwide. It occurs almost everywhere potatoes are grown. In developing countries alone, yield loss due to late blight is estimated to add up to US$ 2.75 billion each year.

The effects of late blight reached disastrous proportions during the Irish Potato Famine of 1845-1851, when it instantly destroyed the primary food source for the majority of the Irish, causing the death of over a million people.

The blight explains the crop failure, but the dramatic and deadly effect of the famine was exacerbated by other factors of economic, political, and social origin.

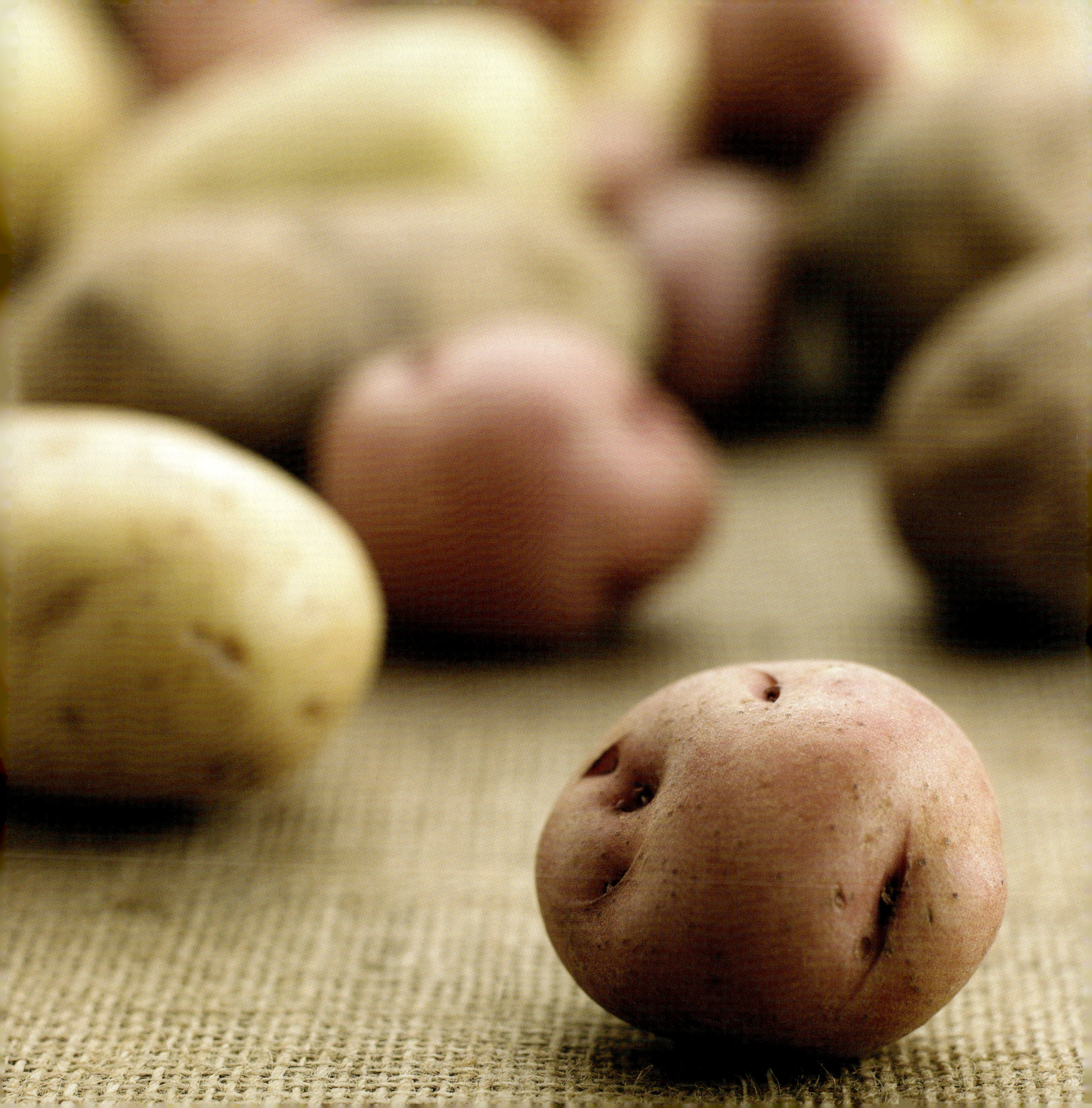

Bratkartoffel – (Fried potatoes)

Preparation time
15 minutes

Cooking time
40 minutes

Serves 4

Difficulty Easy

Ingredients
1 kg potatoes
250g bacon bits
2 onions, peeled and finely chopped
4 tablespoons vegetable oil
salt and pepper

Preparation

The day before, steam or boil the unpeeled potatoes for 25 minutes, drain and set aside to cool at room temperature.

On the day, peel the potatoes and cut them into cubes.

Dry fry (without oil or fat) the bacon bits in a pan until they are crispy, remove with a slotted spoon.

Fry the onions until they are transparent and remove from the pan.

Heat the oil in the pan, add the potatoes and cook until golden brown. Add the onions and bacon bits, add salt and pepper to taste. Mix together and cook for 5 minutes.

Serve hot.

Knödel – (Potato dumplings)

Preparation time
10 minutes

Cooking time
30 minutes

Serves 4

Difficulty Easy

Ingredients
1 kg uncooked potatoes
250g boiled potatoes
350g flour
250ml milk
1 egg
1 packet of small croutons
100g butter
2 tablespoons breadcrumbs
salt, pepper, nutmeg

Preparation

Wash and peel the uncooked potatoes, dry them and grate into a bowl.

Heat the milk and as soon as it boils pour over the grated potatoes. Mix together, then drain the potatoes and place them in a bowl.

Grate the cooked potatoes and add them to the bowl.

Combine the two kinds of potato, flour and egg, salt, pepper and nutmeg and until mix until smooth.

Form into small balls with a crouton in the centre of each.

Poach the knödel in a large pan of boiling water for about 20 minutes. Remove with a slotted spoon and arrange on a serving dish.

In a small pan brown the butter and add the breadcrumbs. Pour over the knödel.

Germany

Knödel are a foundation of German cooking. They are traditionally served with sausages or roast pork.

Potato salad

Preparation time
20 minutes

Cooking time
40 minutes

Serves 4 to 6

Difficulty Easy

Ingredients

1 kg potatoes
1 onion, peeled and chopped
1 stick of celery, washed, trimmed and chopped
250g smoked bacon bits
3 tablespoons vinegar
200ml beef stock
salt and pepper

Germany

Preparation

Steam or boil the unpeeled potatoes for 20 minutes. Drain and peel them and cut into slices. Place in a large salad bowl and add the vinegar.

Mix together the onion and celery.

Dry fry (without oil or fat) the bacon in a pan. Add the onion and celery and cook for 3 minutes. Remove from the heat and add the stock.

Pour the liquid over the potatoes, mix well and add salt and pepper to taste.

Chill for at least 4 hours.

This salad is even better if it's left for 12 hours before being served.

Potato sausages

Preparation time
20 minutes

Cooking time
35 minutes

Serves 4

Difficulty Medium

Ingredients

1 kg potatoes
2 onions, peeled and chopped
250g uncooked sauerkraut
250g smoked bacon bits
3 egg yolks
50g butter
2 tablespoons cream
2 tablespoons flour
4 sprigs of parsley, chopped
salt, pepper, nutmeg

Preparation

Peel and dice the potatoes, steam or cook in boiling salted water for 20 minutes. Drain well and mash.

In a bowl mix together the potatoes, onions, bacon bits, flour, sauerkraut, egg yolks, cream, season with salt, pepper and a little nutmeg.

Shape the mixture into sausages, wrap them tightly in cling-film and set aside to cool.

Melt the butter in a pan. Remove the cling-film and fry the sausages.

Germany

Greek mash

Preparation time
30 minutes

Cooking time
30 minutes

Serves 6

Difficulty Easy

Ingredients

1 kg potatoes
6 garlic cloves, peeled
120g walnuts, roughly chopped
100ml olive oil
juice of 1 lemon
1 bunch of fresh coriander, chopped
salt, pepper and nutmeg

Preparation

Peel and wash the potatoes, cut into chunks and cook them with the whole garlic cloves in boiling salted water for 25 minutes. Drain and mash.

Add the lemon juice and olive oil, a little salt, pepper and nutmeg. Mix together thoroughly.

Transfer to a serving dish, garnish with chopped walnuts and the coriander.

Greece

Greek potato salad

Preparation time
20 minutes

Cooking time
25 minutes

Serves 4

Difficulty Easy

Ingredients

800g firm potatoes

1 red pepper, seeded and cut into fine strips

2 onions, peeled and finely chopped

80ml olive oil

juice of 1 lemon

bunch of flat leaf parsley, chopped

1 tablespoon dry white wine

50g black olives, stoned and sliced

salt and black pepper

Preparation

Steam or cook the unpeeled potatoes in boiling salted water for 25 minutes. Drain, peel and cut into slices. Transfer to a serving dish and pour the white wine over them.

Add the red pepper and parsley to the dish.

Put the onions in a bowl, add the lemon juice and olive oil, season with a little salt and black pepper. Pour over the salad and mix gently.

Garnish with the olives.

Greece

"If you plant the devil's apple, you will be left without wheat and the fields will be starved." In Russia, Tsar Nicholas I suppressed these rumours spread by the peasants by deporting to Siberia the moujiks that refused to cultivate potatoes.

Potato and vegetable briam

Preparation time
20 minutes

Cooking time
30 minutes

Serves 4

Difficulty Medium

Ingredients

2 large potatoes, peeled and cut into bite-sized chunks
2 aubergines
2 courgettes
2 carrots, peeled and sliced
2 green peppers
2 red peppers
1 kg tomatoes
8 mushrooms
2 onions, peeled and chopped
3 garlic cloves, crushed
3 tablespoons olive oil
1 tablespoon tomato concentrate
1 tablespoon vinegar
oil for deep frying
mint leaves, snipped
salt and pepper

Preparation

Wash and dry the aubergines and courgettes, cut into pieces, sprinkle with salt and leave them in a colander to drain for 2 hours.

Peel the potatoes and cut into chunks. Remove the seeds from the peppers and cut into chunks. Peel the tomatoes and remove the seeds.

Rinse the aubergines and courgettes and dry thoroughly. Heat the frying oil, add the aubergines and courgettes and cook for 5 minutes. Remove using a slotted spoon, set aside on kitchen paper. Fry the carrots, potatoes, peppers and mushrooms.

Heat the olive oil in a pan, fry the garlic and onions, then add the fried vegetables, tomatoes, tomato concentrate, vinegar, salt and pepper. Cover and simmer for about 20 minutes or until the vegetables are cooked.

Garnish with the mint.

Serve hot or cold.

Greece

Potato patties with currants

Preparation time
20 minutes

Cooking time
40 minutes

Serves 4 to 6

Difficulty Medium

Ingredients

1 kg potatoes
a sprig of fennel
1 egg
150g currants
200g flour
250g butter
1 tablespoon cumin seeds
1½ tablespoons curry powder
salt

Preparation

Peel the potatoes, place them in a pan filled with cold water, add the fennel, salt and a tablespoon of the curry powder. Cook for 25 minutes.

Drain the potatoes into a bowl and mash them. Add the flour a little at a time together with 150g of the butter. Knead together with the rest of the curry powder and the currants.

Place the dough on a lightly floured surface and roll it out thinly, about 2mm thick. Cut out circles of about 4-6 cm in diameter.

Preheat the oven to 180°C.

Melt the rest of the butter and brush some over a baking sheet. Arrange the patties on the sheet and brush them with melted butter.

Beat the egg and brush over the patties. Sprinkle with cumin seeds.

Bake in the oven for 8 minutes, then turn them over to cook the other side.

Serve hot.

Greece

Skordalia

Preparation time
15 minutes

Cooking time
15 minutes

Serves 4

Difficulty Easy

Ingredients

600g potatoes
3 garlic cloves, crushed
2 tablespoons cider vinegar
60ml olive oil
60g ground almonds
2 slices white bread

Preparation

Peel the potatoes, steam or cook in boiling salted water for 25 minutes.

Cut the crusts off the bread, put the slices in a bowl and add 80ml cold water. Leave for 5 minutes, then squeeze the water out of the bread.

Combine the bread, garlic, almonds and vinegar, then add the olive oil a little at a time.

Mash the potatoes, then stir in the garlic.

Greece

Three-cheese potato gratin

Preparation time
15 minutes

Cooking time
45 minutes

Serves 4

Difficulty Easy

Ingredients

1 kg potatoes
3 garlic cloves, peeled and chopped
200ml crème fraîche
1 teaspoon cayenne pepper
150g goat cheese, thinly sliced
150g cheddar cheese, grated
100g parmesan, grated
30g butter
2 tablespoons oil
salt and pepper

Preparation

Peel and slice the potatoes, steam or cook in boiling salted water for 15 minutes, then drain.

Fry the garlic in the butter, then add the cream, a little salt and pepper and the cayenne pepper.

Preheat the oven to 210°C.

Oil a gratin dish and arrange in it a layer of potato and cover with a layer of cream. Next spread a layer of slices of goat cheese, cover with the rest of the potatoes and then the rest of the cream. Sprinkle with the grated cheeses. Bake in the oven for 30 minutes.

Guatamala

This is also a popular dish in Mexico.

potato

Where are potatoes grown nowadays?

Potatoes can be cultivated everywhere in the world. At one time, potatoes were restricted to cooler climates, but new varieties have been introduced that will grow in almost any part of the world.

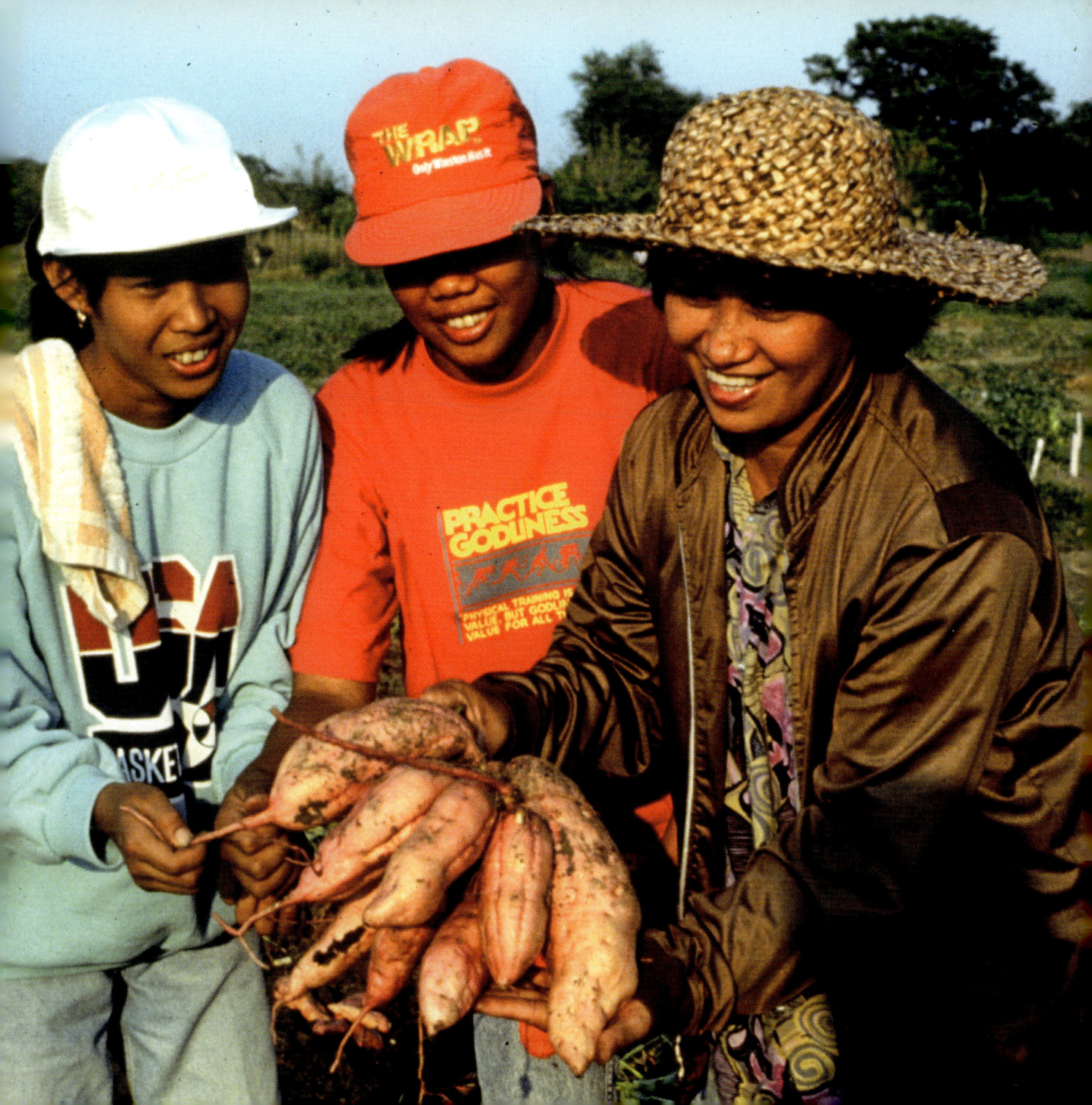
THE WRAP
PRACTICE GODLINESS

Sweet potato bread

Preparation time
15 minutes

Cooking time
1 hour 30 minutes

Serves 4

Difficulty Easy

Ingredients

1 kg sweet potatoes
1 banana
3 eggs
250g sugar
75g butter + 20g for the cake tin
180ml corn syrup
6 tablespoons coconut milk
6 tablespoons condensed milk
4 pinches of ground cinnamon
4 pinches of ground nutmeg
1 teaspoon vanilla extract
50g raisins
salt

Haiti

Preparation

Peel the sweet potatoes and cut into chunks. Cook for 30 minutes in boiling salted water, then drain.

Preheat the oven to 180°C. Butter a cake tin.

In a food processor blend the potatoes, banana, coconut milk, condensed milk, corn syrup, butter, sugar, eggs and spices.

Stir in the raisins.

Transfer to the cake tin and bake in the oven for 1 hour. Leave it to cool down before turning it out of the tin.

Serve warm.

Honduran sopa

Preparation time
15 minutes

Cooking time
1 hour

Serves 4

Difficulty Easy

Ingredients

4 potatoes
2 onions, peeled and chopped
2 chicken stock cubes
150g fresh spinach, trimmed and washed
1 garlic clove, peeled
1 chorizo, sliced
250g chicken escalope
1 teaspoon oregano
1 teaspoon cumin
salt and pepper

Preparation

Fry the chicken in a little hot oil. Add the onions and cook until they are transparent.

Chop the chicken into small chunks and place in a large pan together with the onions, garlic, chorizo and chicken stock cubes. Add 1 litre of hot water, the origano, cumin, salt and pepper, cover and simmer for 35 minutes.

Peel the potatoes and cut them into quarters. Add them to the pan and cook for another 20 minutes. Add the spinach and cook for a few minutes more.

Serve with grated parmesan.

Honduras

Paprika potatoes

Preparation time
30 minutes

Cooking time
1 hour 45 minutes

Serves 4

Difficulty Easy

Ingredients

1 kg potatoes

3 tomatoes, seeded and chopped

500ml chicken stock

3 onions, peeled and finely chopped

1 clove garlic, peeled and finely chopped

1 tablespoon chopped fresh thyme

100g butter

salt, pepper, paprika

Preparation

Peel, rinse and dry the potatoes, then cut into slices.

Melt 100g butter in a large pan and cook the onions, garlic and tomatoes, then add the potatoes. Sprinkle with paprika, add the thyme, season with salt and pepper and mix together well.

Preheat the oven to 180°C.

Transfer the mixture to a oven dish, pour over the stock so that the potatoes are covered. Dot with pieces of butter.

Bake for 1½ hours.

Serve hot.

Hungary

Potatoes with cheddar

Preparation time
20 minutes

Cooking time
1 hour 45 minutes

Serves 4

Difficulty Easy

Ingredients
8 large potatoes
300g cheddar cheese
100g butter
2 tablespoons paprika
salt and pepper

Preparation

Wrap the potatoes in aluminium foil and cook in the oven at 180°C for about 1½ hours or until they are cooked.

Chop the cheddar into small pieces. Melt the butter in a frying pan and add the cheese. Add a little salt, pepper and paprika. Stir until the cheese is melted.

Peel and mash the potatoes, combine with the melted cheese.

Serve hot.

Hungary

Soup with potato balls

Hungary

Preparation time
20 minutes

Cooking time
40 minutes

Serves 4

Difficulty Medium

Ingredients
500g potatoes
1 onion, peeled and chopped
1 litre of beef stock
1 egg
2 tablespoons flour
2 tablespoons crème fraîche
1 bay leaf
1 tablespoon ground cumin
4 sprigs of tarragon
salt

Preparation

Peel and wash the potatoes, and cut them into chunks. Steam or cook in boiling salted water for 25 minutes, then drain and mash them.

Put the onion in a large pan, add the stock, bay leaf, tarragon and cumin. Bring to the boil and cook for 10 minutes.

Beat the egg with the flour and add it to the mashed potatoes. Form small balls with the mixture and poach them in the soup.

Stir the cream into the soup, and serve hot.

The potato occupies an exclusive place among vegetables, for it has the advantage over all "fresh" vegetables of being imperishable. But to prevent a potato from sprouting, turning blue, rotting or withering, it needs to be kept in a dark cool place.

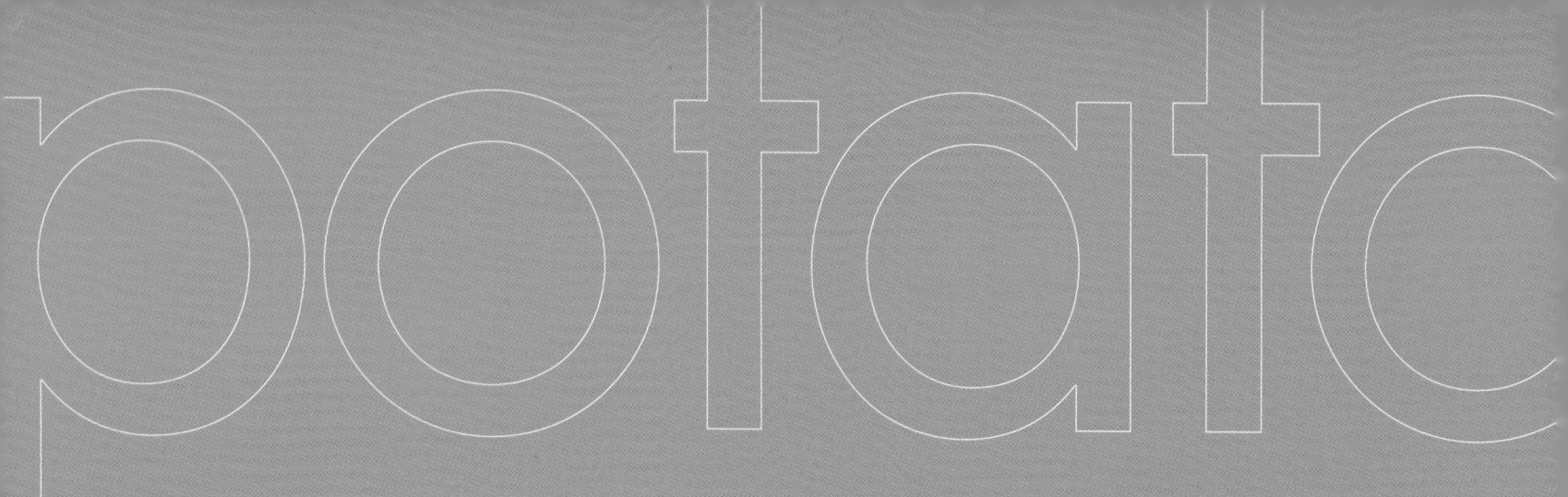

How long does it take to grow potatoes?

It depends on the local climate. In the tropics, farmers can harvest potatoes after 90 days. In colder climates, it can take up to 150 days.

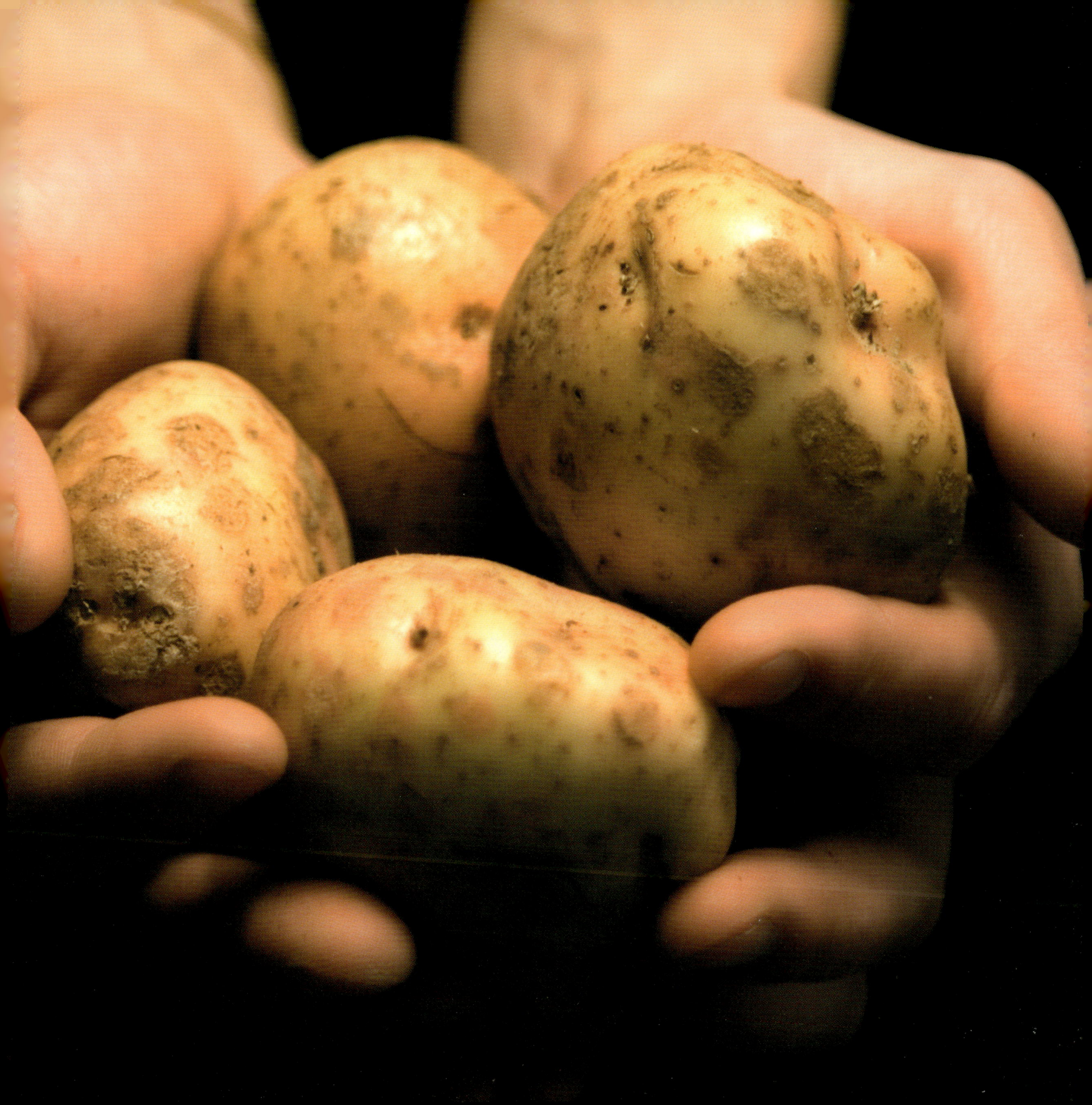

Aloo gobi

Preparation time 20 minutes

Cooking time 30 minutes

Serves 4

Difficulty Easy

Ingredients

500g potatoes

3 garlic cloves, peeled and chopped

1 tomato, skinned, seeded and chopped

2 onions, peeled and chopped

½ cauliflower, separated into small sprigs

bunch of fresh coriander, chopped

½ teaspoon garam masala

1 tablespoon cumin seeds

1 tablespoon mustard seeds

30g clarified butter

salt

India

Preparation

Peel the potatoes and cut them into chunks. Steam or cook in boiling salted water for 10 minutes, then drain.

Dry fry (without oil or fat) the mustard grains in a non-stick frying pan.

Heat the clarified butted, add the mustard grains, cumin, garlic, onion and garam masala. Cook until the onions are tender. Add the tomatoes and cauliflower and cook for another minute.

Bring 250ml water to the boil, add the vegetables, lower the heat and simmer for 15 minutes.

Sprinkle with chopped coriander leaves before serving.

Aloo tikka

Preparation time
20 minutes

Cooking time
35 minutes

Serves 4

Difficulty Easy

Ingredients

800g potatoes
2 green chillies
1 onion, peeled and chopped
a bunch of fresh coriander, chopped
oil for deep frying
salt

Preparation

Peel the potatoes, steam or boil for 25 minutes. Drain and mash.

Remove the seeds from the chillies and chop finely.

Mix the potatoes with the chillies and onion, add a little salt and the chopped coriander leaves.

Form the mixture into small balls.

Heat the oil and drop in the potato cakes. Allow to cook for 6 to 8 minutes. Remove from the oil, and drain on kitchen paper before placing them on a serving dish.

India

Potato processing for the purpose of stimulating our taste buds, and no longer simply as a solution to hunger, began in 1946 with the industrial preparation of crisps and of deep-frozen French fries.

Aubergine and potato curry

Preparation time
20 minutes

Cooking time
40 minutes

Serves 4

Difficulty Easy

Ingredients

600g potatoes

2 aubergines

2 onions, peeled and finely chopped

2 tomatoes, seeded and chopped

2 garlic cloves, peeled and finely chopped

4cm piece of root ginger, peeled and grated

200ml coconut milk

2 tablespoons tomato concentrate

3 tablespoons curry powder

5 tablespoons peanut oil

500ml vegetable stock

5 tablespoons grated coconut

salt

Preparation

Peel the potatoes and cut them into chunks. Cut the aubergines into pieces.

Heat the oil in a pan and fry the onions, garlic and ginger for 5 minutes. Add the aubergines and cook for a further 5 minutes. Sprinkle in the curry powder, then add the tomatoes, potatoes, coconut milk, tomato concentrate and the stock. Mix well, cover and simmer over a gentle heat for 20 minutes.

Transfer to a serving dish and sprinkle with grated coconut.

Serve hot.

India

Potato green massala

Preparation time
15 minutes

Cooking time
30 minutes

Serves 4

Difficulty Easy

Ingredients
1 kg potatoes
200 g frozen peas
1 large onion, peeled and finely chopped
2 garlic cloves, peeled and finely chopped
1 tomato, seeded and chopped
2 tablespoons oil
1 tin unsweetened coconut milk
4 sprigs of coriander, chopped

For the green massala:
2 tablespoons peanut oil
3cm piece of root ginger, peeled and chopped
1 teaspoon fennel seeds
2 whole cloves
1 teaspoon curcuma
2 pods of green cardamom
½ green chilli, seeded
½ teaspoon coriander grains
6 sprigs of coriander, chopped
1 tablespoon ground cinnamon

Preparation

Peel the potatoes, steam or boil them for 25 minutes.

Cut them into cubes.

In a food processor blend the peanut oil with the ginger, chilli, coriander leaves, fennel, whole cloves, curcuma, cinnamon, cardamom grains and coriander grains. Transfer to a pan.

Cook over a gentle heat for 5 minutes stirring all the time. Add the diced potato and cook for another 5 minutes. Remove from the heat and set aside.

Heat the oil in a pan and fry the onion, garlic and tomato for 5 minutes. Add the coconut milk, season with salt and pepper. Cook for another 10 minutes, then add the potatoes and peas. Cook for 5 minutes.

Garnish with the fresh coriander before serving.

India

Saag aloo

Preparation time
30 minutes

Cooking time
60 minutes

Serves 4 to 6

Difficulty Easy

Ingredients

500g potatoes

500g frozen whole spinach

2 onions, peeled and finely chopped

2 garlic cloves, peeled and finely chopped

6 tablespoons vegetable oil

2 teaspoons black mustard seeds

4 pinches cayenne pepper

salt

Preparation

Fill a saucepan with 300ml water, bring to the boil and add the frozen spinach. Cover and leave to cook for about 10 minutes. Drain and rinse in cold water. Squeeze out as much water as possible and set aside in a colander.

Peel the potatoes and cut into cubes.

Heat the oil in a frying pan and add the mustard grains. As soon as they start to jump, add the garlic and onion. Cook on a high heat for 5 minutes stirring all the time. Add the potatoes and spinach. Season with salt and pepper, add 2 tablespoons water and cover. Leave to cook on a low heat for about 40 minutes. When the potatoes are cooked, transfer to a serving dish.

Serve hot.

In India, this dish is served with grilled lamb.

Chicken and potato salad with satay sauce

Preparation time
20 minutes

Cooking time
15 minutes

Serves 4

Difficulty Easy

Ingredients

1 kg potatoes

500g cooked chicken breast

6 small spring onions, finely chopped

12 small fresh spinach leaves, trimmed and chopped

70g unsalted peanuts

150g satay sauce

150g sour cream

Preparation

Steam or boil the potatoes for 25 minutes, then set aside to cool.

Cut the chicken into thin strips.

Peel the potatoes, cut into chunks and place them in a salad bowl. Add the chicken, onions and spinach.

In a small bowl mix together the satay sauce and cream.

Pour over the salad.

Roughly chop the peanuts and sprinkle over the salad.

Indonesia

Gado gado (Mixed vegetables with peanut sauce)

Preparation time
20 minutes

Cooking time
35 minutes

Serves 4

Difficulty Easy

Ingredients

600g potatoes
1 onion, peeled and chopped
1 garlic clove, peeled and chopped
1 carrot, cut into sticks
½ courgette, cut into sticks
100g green beans
100g cauliflower, separated into small sprigs
2 tablespoons vegetable oil
½ teaspoon ground pimento
3 tablespoons peanut butter
juice of 1 lime
2 tablespoons unsalted peanuts
salt and pepper

Preparation

Steam or boil the unpeeled potatoes for 25 minutes. Set aside to cool, then peel and slice them.

Cook the green beans for 10 minutes in boiling salted water, drain and set aside to cool.

Combine the peanut butter and lime juice. Add the pimento, oil, salt and pepper, and add a little water so that the sauce coats the back of a spoon. Stir in the garlic and onion.

Place all the vegetables in a serving dish, pour over the sauce and garnish with crushed peanuts.

This dish can be prepared using other vegetables: tomato, cucumber, green cabbage, cress...

Indonesia

Pooreh seeb zamini

Preparation time
10 minutes

Cooking time
20 minutes

Serves 4

Difficulty Easy

Ingredients
1 kg potatoes
250ml milk
30g butter
salt

Preparation

Peel and wash the potatoes, cut them into chunks and put them in a pan. Add 2 glasses of water, season with salt and cook over a low heat for 20 minutes. Drain them.

Mash the potatoes with a fork. Add the milk slowly while stirring so that the milk is fully absorbed by the potatoes.

Add butter, mix well, and serve hot.

Iran

Champ

Preparation time
5 minutes

Cooking time
25 minutes

Serves 4

Difficulty Easy

Ingredients

800g potatoes
110g spring onions, chopped
350ml milk
100g butter
salt and pepper

Ireland

Preparation

Steam or boil the unpeeled potatoes for 20 minutes.

Place the onions in a pan and cover with milk. Bring to the boil and simmer for 4 minutes. Remove from the heat and set aside.

Peel the potatoes, mash them and add the onions and milk. Mix in the butter, season with salt and pepper and serve hot.

This dish is a favourite with the Irish who, of course, are the champion consumers of potatoes in Europe.

Colcannon

Preparation time
20 minutes

Cooking time
45 minutes

Serves 4

Difficulty Easy

Ingredients

1 kg potatoes

500g green cabbage, shredded

2 leeks, trimmed, washed and cut into thin strips

100ml milk

100g butter, chopped into small pieces

salt and pepper

Preparation

Peel and rinse the potatoes, cut into chunks, steam or cook in boiling salted water for 20 minutes. Drain and mash

Rinse the cabbage and cook in boiling salted water for 15 minutes, then drain.

Place the leeks in a pan, cover with milk and cook until tender.

Add the cabbage to the potatoes, together with the leeks and milk. Combine well, check the seasoning and add the butter.

Serve hot.

Ireland

This dish is traditionally served at Halloween.

Dublin coddle

Preparation time
20 minutes

Cooking time
1 hour 30 minutes

Serves 4

Difficulty Easy

Ingredients

750g potatoes
2 carrots, peeled and sliced
2 onions, peeled and chopped
4 sausages
4 slices of bacon
30g butter
2 whole cloves
1 bouquet garni
200ml cider
salt and pepper

Preparation

Peel the potatoes, wash and dry them and cut them into chunks.

Melt the butter in a pan and cook the onions for 5 minutes. Add the potatoes, carrots, bouquet garni, cloves, season with salt and pepper. Cover with the cider and leave to simmer for 1½ hours.

Fry the bacon and the sausages.

Transfer the vegetables to a serving dish, and garnish with the bacon and sausages.

Ireland

Irish stew

Preparation time
20 minutes

Cooking time
2 hours 30 minutes

Serves 4 to 6

Difficulty Easy

Ingredients

1½ kg potatoes

600g slices neck of mutton

600g mutton spare ribs

1 stick celery, washed, trimmed and chopped

¼ green cabbage, chopped

4 large onions, peeled and chopped

1 bouquet garni

salt and pepper

Preparation

Peel the potatoes and cut into slices about ½ cm thick. Mix together the potatoes, onions, celery and cabbage, season with salt and pepper.

Preheat the oven to 180°C.

In a large casserole dish put a layer of vegetables, add a layer of meat, season with salt and pepper, add the rest of the vegetables and the bouquet garni, and enough water to cover.

Close the dish tightly and bake for 2½ hours. Remove the bouquet garni before serving.

Ireland

Irish stew is the national dish of Ireland.

Potato scones

Preparation time
20 minutes

Cooking time
45 minutes

Serves 4

Difficulty Easy

Ingredients
300g potatoes
400g flour
200ml milk
125g grated cheese
30g butter
salt

Ireland

Preparation

Peel the potatoes and cut them into chunks. Steam or boil for 25 minutes, then drain and mash them in a large bowl, season with salt.

Melt the butter.

Add the flour to the potatoes and knead them together. Add the milk and melted butter and mix well.

Preheat the oven to 210°C.

Roll the dough into a long sausage and cut it into slices.

Arrange the scones on a buttered baking tray. Sprinkle with grated cheese.

Bake in the oven for 20 minutes.

Serve hot.

Latkes (potato pancakes)

Preparation time
15 minutes

Cooking time
15 minutes

Serves 4

Difficulty Easy

Ingredients
1 kg potatoes
1 large onion, peeled and chopped
2 eggs
50g polenta
80 ml vegetable oil
salt and pepper

To serve:
100g apple sauce
2 tablespoons sour cream

Preparation

Peel the potatoes and grate them. Squeeze out the excess moisture and place in a salad bowl.

Beat the eggs, season with salt and pepper.

Add to the potatoes the onion, polenta and eggs. Mix well. Divide the mixture into 12 and form each into a small pancake.

Heat the oil in a pan. Cook the pancakes until golden brown, then turn them over. When the other side is golden brown take them out and drain on kitchen paper.

Serve with sour cream and apple sauce.

Israel

Latkes are traditionally eaten during the Jewish Hanukkah festival, as a reminder of the miraculous oil.

Potato ravioli

Preparation time
40 minutes

Cooking time
40 minutes

Serves 6

Difficulty Medium

Ingredients

750g potatoes
600g flour
3 eggs
1 onion, peeled and chopped
50g butter
salt and pepper

Israel

Preparation

Put the flour in a large bowl, make a well in the centre and add a pinch of salt, 2 of the eggs and 100ml water. Knead the dough until smooth and form it into a ball. Roll out the dough on a lightly floured surface and cut out circles.

Steam or boil the unpeeled potatoes for 25 minutes. Peel and mash them using half the butter, season with salt and pepper.

Fry the onions gently in a knob of butter. Stir them into the mashed potato together with the remaining egg, beaten.

Put a spoonful of mash in the centre of each circle of dough, fold over and seal the edges firmly.

Poach the ravioli in boiling water until they rise to the surface. Drain on kitchen paper. Serve with melted butter.

Frittata

Preparation time
15 minutes

Cooking time
40 minutes

Serves 4

Difficulty Easy

Ingredients
1 kg potatoes
10 eggs
1 red pepper
1 yellow pepper
100g mozzarella, diced
4 tablespoons olive oil
salt and pepper

Preparation

Steam or boil the unpeeled potatoes for 25 minutes, drain and peel them.

Skin the peppers, discard the seeds and cut into strips.

Heat 2 tablespoons of oil in a large frying pan and cook the peppers for about 10 minutes.

In a large bowl beat the eggs, season with salt and pepper, and add the peppers, potatoes and mozzarella.

Heat the rest of the oil and pour in the omelette mixture. Cook over a low heat for about 10 minutes without stirring. As soon as the frittata is golden brown, slide it on to an oven-proof dish and put it under a medium hot grill until the top is browned.

Italy

Potato gnocchi

Preparation time
25 minutes

Cooking time
35 minutes

Serves 4

Difficulty Easy

Ingredients
1 kg potatoes
100g flour
3 egg yolks
20g butter
4 tablespoons grated parmesan cheese
salt and pepper

Italy

Preparation

Peel the potatoes, cut into chunks, steam or cook them in boiling salted water for about 20 minutes. Mash and place in a large bowl.

Add the flour, egg yolks, season with a little salt and pepper.

Take small quantities of dough and roll into small balls.

Fill a large pan with salted water and bring to the boil, lower the heat slightly and drop in the gnocchi. Remove with a slotted spoon as soon as they rise to the surface. Drain and place in a buttered oven dish.

Preheat the oven to 240°.

Sprinkle with parmesan and bake for about 10 minutes.

Serve with a tomato sauce.

Potatoes stuffed with mascarpone

Preparation time
10 minutes

Cooking time
40 minutes

Serves 4

Difficulty Easy

Ingredients

4 large potatoes

60g Parma ham, chopped

60g mascarpone or crème fraîche

1 bunch of chives, chopped

25g butter

a pinch of nutmeg

salt and pepper

Preparation

Steam or boil the unpeeled potatoes for 25–30 minutes. Drain them and set aside to cool.

Preheat the oven to 180°C.

Scoop the pulp out of the potatoes taking care not to pierce the outer skin. Put the pulp in a bowl and add the mascarpone, ham, chives, season with salt and pepper.

Fill the potato cases with the mixture and add a knob of butter on top of each. Place them in an oven dish and bake in the oven for 10 minutes.

Serve hot.

Italy

Potatoes with artichokes (Sardinia)

Preparation time 15 minutes

Cooking time 20 minutes

Serves 4

Difficulty Easy

Ingredients

600g potatoes
4 cooked artichoke bottoms
2 garlic cloves, peeled and chopped
3 tablespoons olive oil
4 sprigs of flat leaf parsley, chopped
salt and pepper

Italy

Preparation

Peel the potatoes and cut into cubes.

Rinse the artichoke bottoms, dry and cut into pieces.

Heat the oil in a pan, add the garlic and parsley, then the artichoke and potato cubes. Season with salt and pepper. Fry for 5 minutes until golden brown, then add 250ml water.

Cover the pan and simmer for 20 minutes over a low heat.

Serve hot.

If the potatoes dry up, add a little more water.

Tiella

Preparation time
30 minutes

Cooking time
1 hour 30 minutes

Serves 4 to 6

Difficulty Medium

Ingredients

800g potatoes

450g aubergines

800g tomatoes, skinned and seeded

2 stalks celery, washed, trimmed and chopped

1 onion, peeled and finely chopped

2 garlic cloves, peeled and finely chopped

4 sprigs of parsley, chopped

2 tablespoons dried oregano

60ml olive oil

2 tablespoons coarse salt

Preparation

Wash and dry the aubergines, remove the stalk and cut into thin slices. Sprinkle with coarse salt and leave to give up their liquid for 30 minutes. Rinse and dry on kitchen paper.

Preheat the oven to 180°C. Grease a gratin dish.

Cut the tomatoes into small chunks and place in a bowl with the onion, garlic, celery, parsley and oregano.

Peel and rinse the potatoes and cut into thin slices. Dry on kitchen paper. Put half the potato in the oven dish, cover with half the aubergines and half the vegetable mixture and drizzle with a little olive oil. Repeat with the rest of the ingredients.

Cover with a sheet of aluminium foil and bake in the oven for 1½ hours.

Serve hot.

Italy

This dish originates from the region of Apulia, in the south-east of Italy.

Which spirit is distilled from potatoes?

Vodka is distilled from potatoes. Less famously, aquavit is also a potato-based liquor.

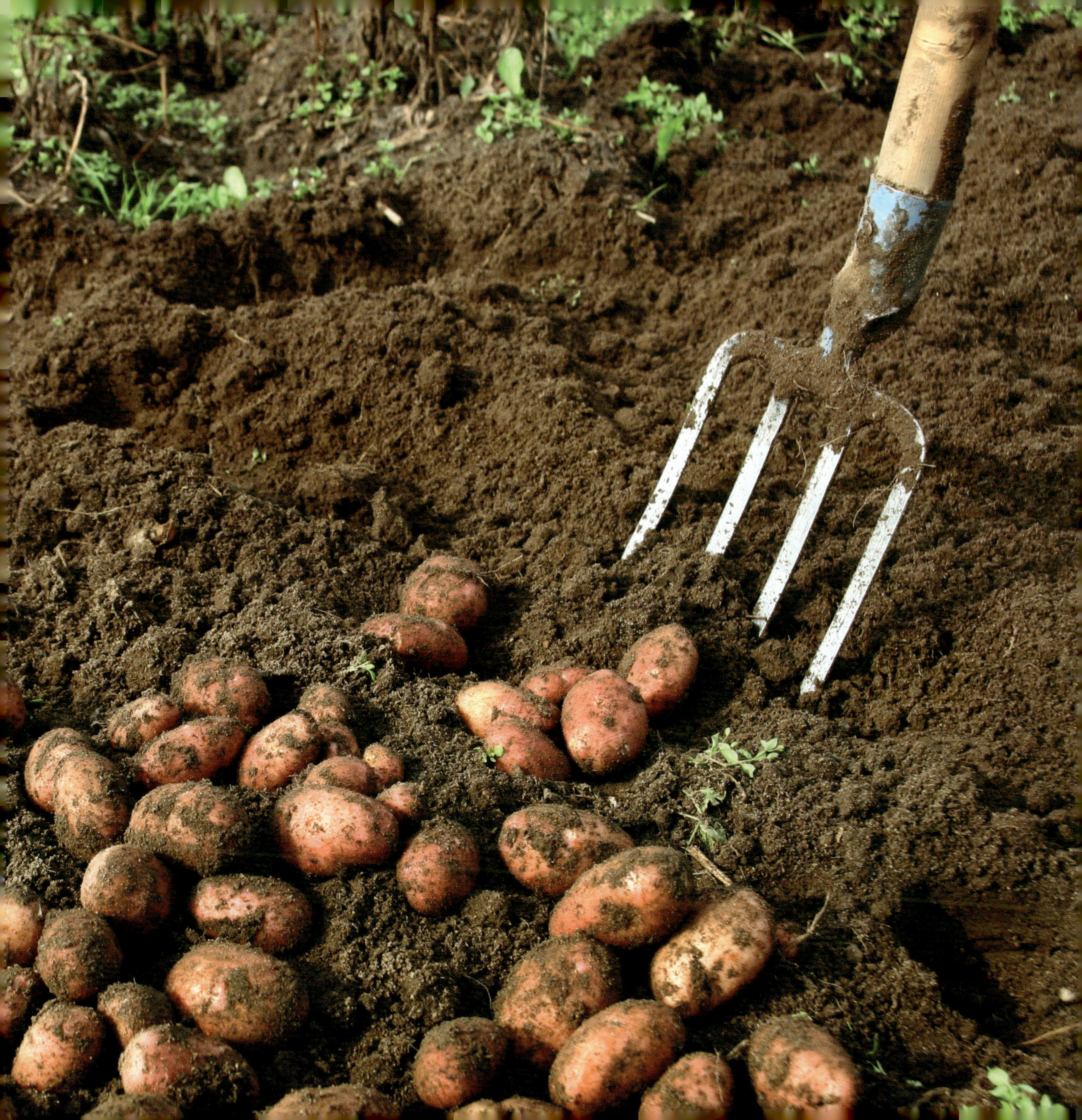

Spicy sweet potatoes

Preparation time
10 minutes

Cooking time
20 minutes

Serves 4

Difficulty Easy

Ingredients

1 kg sweet potatoes
2 garlic cloves, peeled and chopped
4cm piece of root ginger, grated
2 teaspoons Jamaican pimento
1 teaspoon cayenne pepper
2 teaspoons chopped thyme
2 tablespoons oil
30g butter
salt

Preparation

Peel and dice the sweet potatoes.

Heat the oil and butter in a pan, add the sweet potatoes and cook them for 10 minutes stirring all the time.

Add the garlic, ginger, spices and thyme, and continue cooking for 10 minutes.

Serve hot.

Jamaica

Shingjagaimo

Preparation time
15 minutes

Cooking time
15 minutes

Serves 4

Difficulty Easy

Ingredients

8 new potatoes
2 small cucumbers
6 teaspoons sesame oil
6 teaspoons soy sauce
4 teaspoons Japanese rice vinegar
½ teaspoon rice syrup
½ teaspoon karashi mustard

Preparation

Bring a pan of water to the boil.

Combine the soy sauce, rice vinegar, rice syrup, mustard and sesame oil.

Peel the potatoes, cut into small sticks, rinse, and drop into the boiling water.

When the water reboils, cook for 10 seconds, drain and set aside to cool.

Peel the cucumbers and remove the seeds. Cut them into sticks the same size as the potatoes.

When the potatoes are cold, in a bowl mix the potatoes and cucumber strips together, then pour the sauce over the vegetables. Let the dish marinate for a few minutes.

Serve at room temperature.

Japan

Sweet potato croquettes

Preparation time
30 minutes

Cooking time
35 minutes

Serves 4

Difficulty Easy

Ingredients

800g sweet potatoes

2 stalks of lemon grass, chopped coarsely

2 garlic cloves, peeled and finely chopped

4 tablespoons olive oil

3cm piece of root ginger, peeled and chopped

1 small chilli, seeded and chopped

400g pink shrimps, peeled and chopped

½ bunch basil, chopped

½ bunch coriander, chopped

1 egg yolk

6 tablespoons Japanese breadcrumbs

oil for deep frying

salt and pepper

Japan

Preparation

Peel and chop the sweet potatoes.

Heat 2 tablespoons of olive oil in a large pan and fry the garlic and lemon grass for 5 minutes. Add the sweet potatoes, salt and pepper, and 100ml water. Leave to cook for 25 minutes.

Combine the ginger, chilli, basil, coriander and shrimps.

Mash the sweet potatoes with a fork. Add the shrimp mixture and 2 tablespoons of olive oil. Place the potato into a piping bag fitted with a large nozzle and pipe croquettes about 4cm long on to a greased baking tray. Put them in the freezer for 1 hour.

Beat the egg yolk in a shallow dish, and put the breadcrumbs in another. Dip the croquettes into the egg, then roll them in the breadcrumbs.

Heat the frying oil and deep fry the croquettes for a few minutes. They should be golden brown. Drain on kitchen paper.

Serve hot.

Japanese breadcrumbs are lighter and crunchier than ordinary breadcrumbs. They can be found in Asian grocery stores.

Sweet potatoes with tomatoes

Preparation time
10 minutes

Cooking time
15 minutes

Serves 4

Difficulty Easy

Ingredients

4 sweet potatoes
4 small tomatoes
tablespoon olive oil
2 pinches of ground pimento
salt and pepper

Preparation

Peel the sweet potatoes and cut into slices 1cm thick. Cook them in boiling salted water for 7 minutes. Drain them well and dry on kitchen paper.

Heat the oil in a pan and fry the potato slices, turning them over regularly. Drain them and arrange on a serving dish, adding a little salt and pepper.

Cut the tomato into slices and garnish the potatoes with them. Sprinkle a little pimento over the top.

Kenya

potato

Is it difficult to cultivate potatoes?

No. The potato is easy to deal with, reliable and inexhaustible as it is. It can even regenerate of its own accord and does so with great vigour. It is also cultivated all over the world, on different continents and under different climates.

Good-natured though it is, the potato is nonetheless vulnerable. It thoroughly dislikes frost and seasons that are either too wet or too dry.

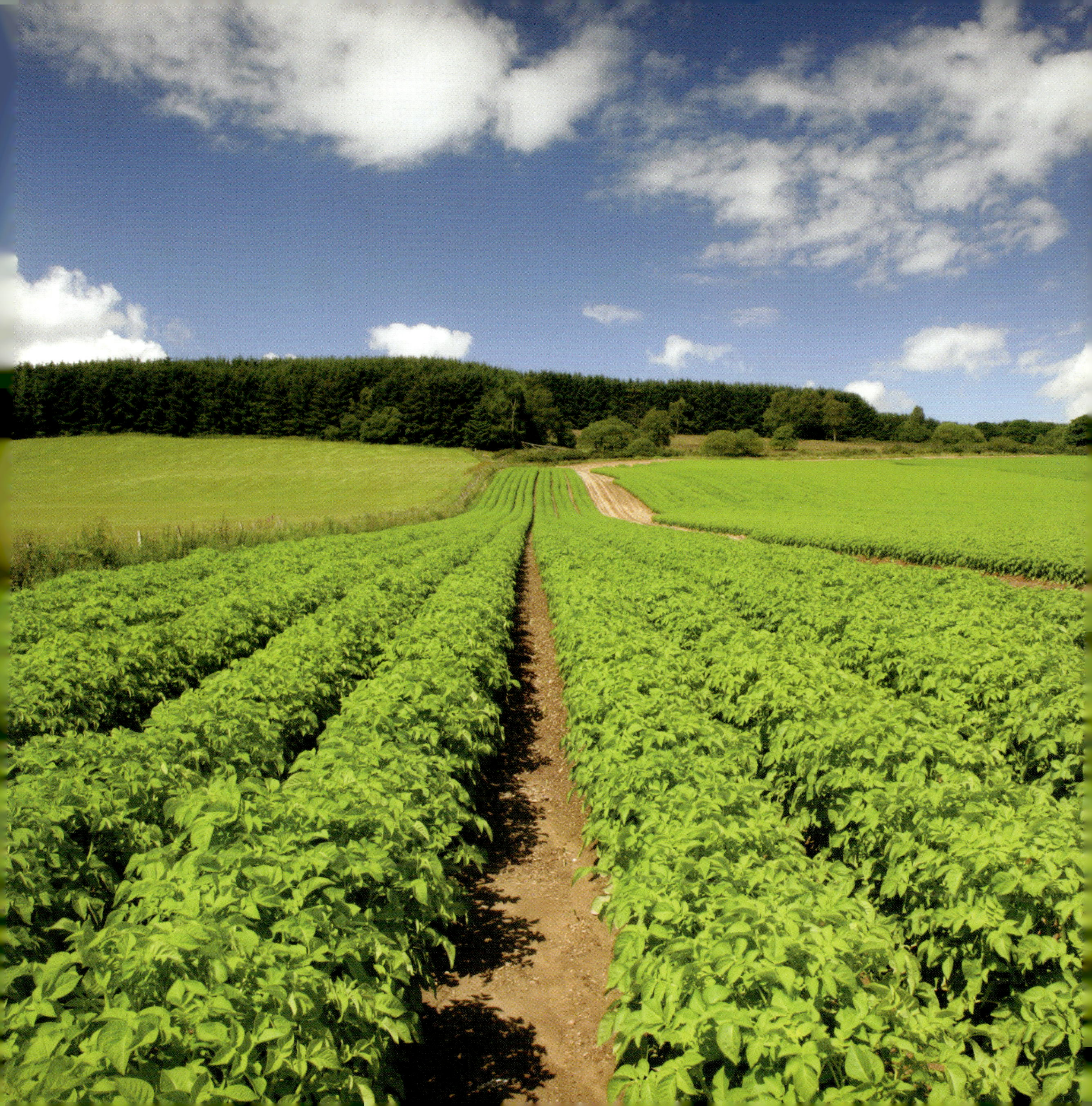

Livonian herrings

Preparation time
15 minutes

Cooking time
25 minutes

Serves 4

Difficulty Easy

Ingredients

8 small potatoes
8 smoked herring fillets
2 reinette apples, peeled and diced
1 fennel bulb, finely chopped
2 sprigs of chervil, chopped
2 sprigs of tarragon, chopped
2 tablespoons vinegar
5 tablespoons vegetable oil

Preparation

Steam or boil the unpeeled potatoes for 25 minutes. Peel them and cut them into pieces.

Cut the herring fillets into sticks.

Put the potatoes in a bowl and add the herring, apples and fennel.

Whisk together the vinegar and oil, and pour them over the salad. Garnish with chervil and tarragon.

Latvia

Herb potatoes

Preparation time
15 minutes

Cooking time
15 minutes

Serves 4

Difficulty Easy

Ingredients

1 kg potatoes
2 garlic cloves, crushed
1 large bunch flat leaf parsley, chopped
1 small bunch fresh coriander, chopped
2 tablespoons olive oil
oil for deep frying
salt and freshly ground pepper

Preparation

Peel and rinse the potatoes, cut into slices ½ cm thick.

Deep fry in frying oil.

In a pan, fry the garlic in a little olive oil until slightly coloured. Add the herbs. Mix together and pour over the potatoes.

Lebanon

The great French defender of the potato, Antoine Augustin Parmentier (1737-1813) gave a masterful demonstration in 1785, when he organized a dinner in honour of the scientists Lavoisier and Benjamin Franklin, based entirely on potatoes.

Potato stew

Preparation time
20 minutes

Cooking time
1 hour 15 minutes

Serves 4 to 6

Difficulty Easy

Ingredients

1kg potatoes

600g beef shank on the bone, cut into large chunks

2 onions, peeled and finely chopped

3 garlic cloves, peeled and finely chopped

1 litre tomato juice

2 tablespoons clarified butter

3 tablespoons peanut oil

salt and pepper

Preparation

Peel the potatoes and cut into large chunks. Fry in the oil until golden brown and set aside.

Cut the meat into large chunks.

Heat the clarified butter in a pan sear seize the meat. Add the onion and garlic, season with salt and pepper and cook for 10 minutes.

Add the tomato juice, bring to the boil and leave to simmer until the meat is completely cooked.

Transfer the potatoes to the pan and continue cooking for 20 minutes.

Serve hot.

Potatoes in oil

Preparation time
30 minutes

Cooking time
60 minutes

Serves 4

Difficulty Easy

Ingredients

1kg potatoes
2 tomatoes, cut into small chunks
2 large onions, chopped
6 garlic cloves, peeled and chopped
1 green chilli, seeded and chopped
2 tablespoons olive oil
2 tablespoons peanut oil
oil for deep frying
salt and pepper

Preparation

Peel the potatoes and cut into slices ½ cm thick.

Fry the potatoes in the frying oil, being careful not to overcook.

Drain.

In a pan, add the olive oil and peanut oil, fry the garlic and onions until coloured.

Add the tomato, chilli and potatoes, season with salt and pepper.

Simmer on a low heat for 10 minutes and allow to cool.

Serve cold.

Lebanon

Sweet potato cake

Preparation time
10 minutes

Cooking time
40 minutes

Serves 4

Difficulty Easy

Ingredients

300g sweet potatoes
4 tablespoons brown sugar
2 teaspoons ground ginger
2 teaspoons dried yeast
4 tablespoons oil
1 tablespoon oil for the cake pan
salt

Liberia

Preparation

Peel and grate the sweet potatoes. Mix in the ginger, yeast, brown sugar and a little salt.

Heat the oil in a pan, add the potatoes and cook for 10 minutes, stirring all the time.

Preheat the oven to 180°C.

Oil a cake pan. Transfer the mixture to the pan and bake in the oven for 30 minutes.

Cut the cake into squares and serve hot or cold.

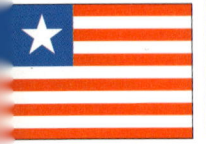

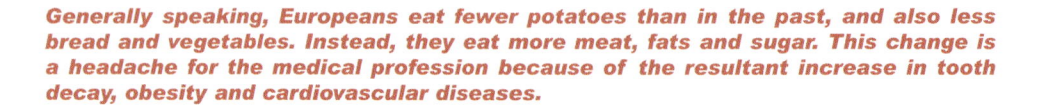

Generally speaking, Europeans eat fewer potatoes than in the past, and also less bread and vegetables. Instead, they eat more meat, fats and sugar. This change is a headache for the medical profession because of the resultant increase in tooth decay, obesity and cardiovascular diseases.

Tajin bel Hut (Mullet and potato tagine)

Preparation time
15 minutes

Cooking time
20 minutes

Serves 4

Difficulty Easy

Ingredients

4 potatoes
4 whole mullet
2 tomatoes, skinned, seeded and chopped
1 onion, peeled and finely chopped
juice of 1 lemon
1 stick of celery, washed, trimmed and chopped
2 red chillies, seeded and finely chopped
2 garlic cloves, peeled and finely chopped
1 tablespoon cumin
1 tablespoon paprika
4 tablespoons olive oil
salt

Preparation

Gut the fish, scale and wash them.

Peel and wash the potatoes, cut them into pieces.

Heat the oil in a pot and fry the garlic, onion, celery, chillies and tomato for 5 minutes. Add the potatoes and stir together. Place the mullet on the vegetables, sprinkle with cumin and paprika, cover the pot and cook over a gentle heat for 10 minutes.

Add the lemon juice and continue cooking until the sauce thickens.

Serve hot.

Libyan Arab Jamahiriya

Blynai is virtu bulviu

Preparation time
15 minutes

Cooking time
40 minutes

Serves 4

Difficulty Easy

Ingredients

800g potatoes
2 tablespoons flour
4 eggs, beaten
6 tablespoons breadcrumbs
100g butter
salt and pepper

Preparation

Peel the potatoes, cut them into pieces, steam or cook in boiling salted water for 25 minutes. Drain and mash them.

Add the flour and eggs, and a little salt and pepper.

Form small pancakes and roll them in the breadcrumbs.

Melt the butter in a large pan until it sizzles, then cook the pancakes for a few minutes so that both sides are golden brown.

Serve hot with cream.

Lithuania

Cepelinai

Preparation time
30 minutes

Cooking time
50 minutes

Serves 4

Difficulty Medium

Ingredients

1 kg potatoes
70g minced pork
1 onion, peeled and chopped
1 tablespoon oil
salt and pepper

Preparation

Steam or boil 250g potatoes, unpeeled, for 25 minutes. Peel and mash them.

Peel and grate the remaining potatoes, squeezing out the excess liquid. Knead together the two sorts of potato and season with salt and pepper.

Fry the onion in a tablespoon of oil, then mix with the meat.

Take 2 tablespoons of the potato mixture at a time and make flattened oval patties. Place spoonfuls of the meat filling into the centre of the patties and then close them around the meat, making a dumpling shape.

Poach the patties in boiling salted water for 25 minutes. Remove them with a slotted spoon and drain on kitchen paper.

Serve hot.

Lithuania

Serve with melted butter, or cream mixed with tomato concentrate.

Kugelis

Preparation time
15 minutes

Cooking time
1 hour 10 minutes

Serves 4

Difficulty Easy

Ingredients

1 kg potatoes
1 onion, peeled and finely chopped
500g bacon bits
8 eggs, beaten
2 tablespoons flour
1 tin condensed milk
salt and pepper

Lithuania

Preparation

Dry fry (without oil or fat) the bacon bits and onion in a pan.

Peel, wash and dry the potatoes. Grate them into a bowl.

Melt the butter and add this to the potatoes. Add the onion, bacon, eggs, flour, condensed milk and a little salt and pepper. Mix together well.

Preheat the oven to 180°C.

Transfer the mixture to a buttered oven dish. Bake in the oven for 1 hour.

Cut it into pieces and serve with cream.

Potato and sauerkraut pancakes

Preparation time
20 minutes

Cooking time
35 minutes

Serves 4

Difficulty Medium

Ingredients

750g potatoes
500g cooked sauerkraut
100g smoked bacon, diced
50g butter
salt and pepper

Preparation

Steam or boil the unpeeled potatoes for 25 minutes, peel and mash them.

Add the sauerkraut, season with salt and pepper and mix thoroughly.

Dry fry (without oil or fat) the bacon in a pan, then add to the vegetables.

Roll the mash out on a lightly floured surface and use a cutter to cut out small thick pancakes.

Melt the butter in a large pan and fry the pancakes on both sides until golden brown.

Serve hot.

Luxembourg

Victor Hugo nicknamed the potato the "poor man's truffle" in his work **Les Misérables.**

potato

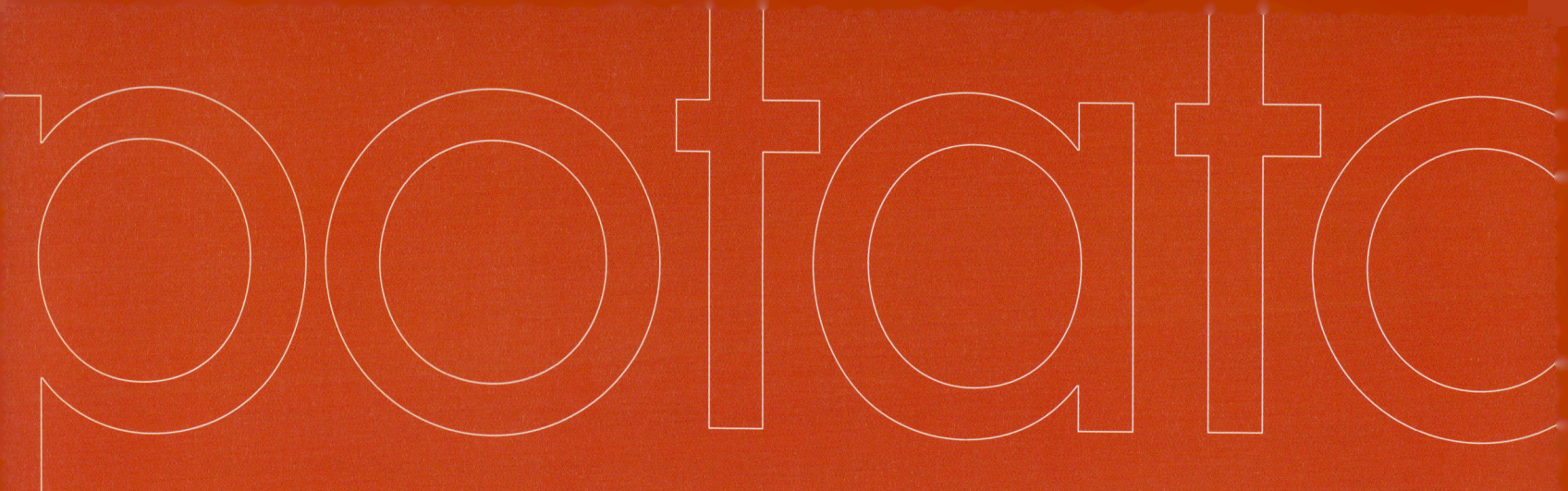

How was the potato treated when it first arrived in Europe?

The potato was given rather a mixed reception. It aroused the interest of scientists who were fascinated by its regenerative virtues. It also stirred the curiosity of royalty who granted it a place in their gardens. On the other hand, the masses shunned it with suspicion and hostility and cursed it as an evil food.

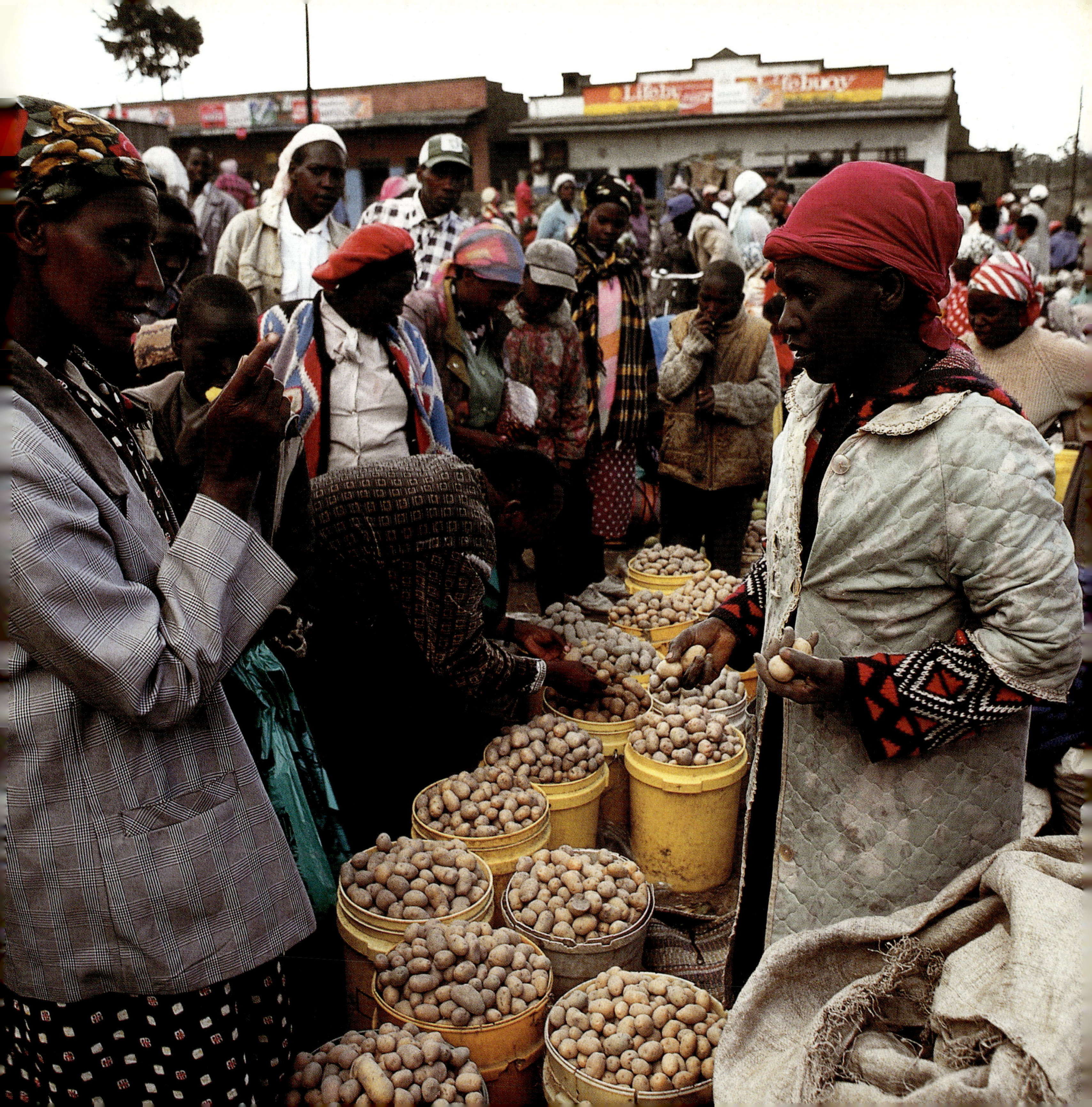

Lasopy tongotr'omby

Preparation time
10 minutes

Cooking time
4 hours

Serves 4

Difficulty Easy

Ingredients

4 potatoes
2 tomatoes
250g white beans
1 beef shank (approx. 1½ kg)
salt

Preparation

Put the beef shank in a cooking pot, add 3 litres of salted water and the white beans.

Bring to the boil, then lower the heat and simmer for 3 hours, skimming the surface often.

Peel the potatoes and cut them into pieces. Peel the tomatoes, remove the seeds and cut them into quarters. Add the potatoes and tomatoes to the cooking pot and simmer for a further hour. Check the seasoning and serve hot.

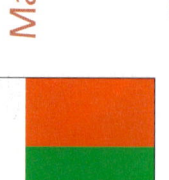

Madagascar

Mbatata cookies

Preparation time
10 minutes

Cooking time
45 minutes

Serves 4

Difficulty Easy

Ingredients

800g sweet potatoes
200ml milk
100g butter
150g flour, sifted
2 teaspoons yeast
4 tablespoons sugar
1 teaspoon ground cinnamon
salt

Preparation

Peel the sweet potatoes, cook in boiling salted water for 30 minutes. Drain and mash them.

Mix the potatoes with the milk and butter. Add the flour, yeast and a little salt and mix well.

Preheat the oven to 180°C.

Spoon the mixture into a cookie tin and bake in the oven for 15 minutes. Remove from the tin and sprinkle with the sugar and cinnamon.

Malawi

Symptoms of the potato blight were first recorded in Belgium in 1845. Plant pathologist Jean Beagle Ristanio speculates that the pathogen (not a fungus but an oomycete) arrived in Europe on a shipment of potatoes from South America in the 1830s. Europe's entire potato crop soon fell victim to the fungal infection, none more so than in Ireland.

Patata l-Forn (Oven baked potatoes)

Preparation time
10 minutes

Cooking time
25 minutes

Serves 6

Difficulty Easy

Ingredients

1.2 kg yellow fleshy potatoes, peeled and sliced not thicker than 1 cm

400g red onion, peeled and sliced into thin rings

2 garlic cloves, roughly chopped

2 tsp fennel seeds, lightly crushed in a mortar (cumin can be used instead)

3 tbs good cooking oil

1 wine glass of water or stock

Salt and pepper, ideally coarsely ground

Preparation

Preheat the oven to 150° C.

Arrange the potatoes and onions in layers in an oven dish and add all the other ingredients, season with salt and pepper. Add a glass of stock and sprinkle some pepper over the top.

Cook in the oven for about 25 minutes or until done – use a sharp fork to test. When ready the top layer should be beautifully browned and the onion caramelised.

If meat is also being cooked, place the potatoes and onions around the joint and add a glass of water instead of stock.

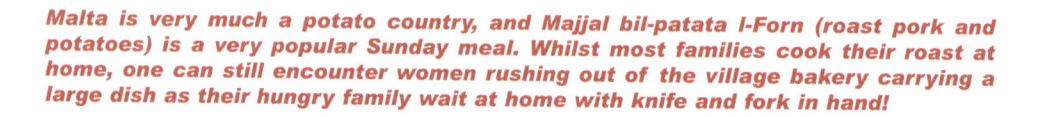

Malta is very much a potato country, and Majjal bil-patata l-Forn (roast pork and potatoes) is a very popular Sunday meal. Whilst most families cook their roast at home, one can still encounter women rushing out of the village bakery carrying a large dish as their hungry family wait at home with knife and fork in hand!

Malta

Potato dizef curry

Preparation time
15 minutes

Cooking time
30 minutes

Serves 6

Difficulty Easy

Ingredients

1 kg new potatoes
12 hard-boiled eggs, peeled
5 tomatoes
1 onion, peeled and chopped
2 garlic cloves, peeled and chopped
3cm piece of root ginger, peeled and chopped
1 tablespoon ground coriander
1 tablespoon cinnamon
1 tablespoon fennel seeds
2 whole cloves
2 cardamom pods
1 pinch of saffron strands
1 bunch of coriander
250ml olive oil
salt and pepper

Preparation

Peel and wash the potatoes, cut them into chunks.

Fry the potatoes in hot oil until they are tender, then remove them from the pan.

Mix together the spices and add a glass of water. Combine with the onions, garlic and ginger. Add the tomatoes to the potatoes and heat through.

Arrange the potatoes and hard-boiled eggs on a serving dish and pour the sauce over them. Garnish with chopped coriander.

Mauritius

Potato soup

Preparation time
10 minutes

Cooking time
30 minutes

Serves 6

Difficulty Easy

Ingredients

600g potatoes
2 onions, peeled and chopped
1 litre milk
1 sprig of parsley, chopped
1 teaspoon chopped thyme
75g grated cheese
25g butter
salt and pepper

Mauritius

Preparation

Peel the potatoes, wash them and cut them into chunks.

Melt the butter in a large pan. Add the onions and potatoes and cook for 20 minutes. Season with salt and pepper, then blend them in a food processor.

Put them back in the pan and add the milk. Heat the mixture and add the grated cheese, together with the thyme and parsley. As soon as the cheese is melted, remove from the heat.

Serve hot.

Potato and bean salad

Preparation time
20 minutes

Cooking time
25 minutes

Serves 4

Difficulty Easy

Ingredients

1 kg small potatoes
300g cooked beans
1 small red pepper
1 avocado
1 small chilli
2 garlic cloves
1 onion
80g sour cream
4 sprigs of parsley
4 sprigs of fresh coriander
1 packet corn fritters
1 tablespoon lemon juice
2 tablespoons vegetable oil
salt and pepper

Preparation

Steam or boil the potatoes for 25 minutes. Peel and chop into chunks.

Remove the seeds from the red pepper and the chilli, and chop into small cubes. Peel the avocado and cut into cubes. Put all these vegetables into a bowl.

Chop together the onion and garlic with the parsley and coriander. Put them in a bowl and add the oil, lemon juice, cream, salt and pepper. Combine well and pour the mixture over the salad.

After deseeding the chilli, wash your hands thoroughly, as the oil in the seed and pith can burn the skin and eyes.

Mexico

Stuffed potatoes

Preparation time
25 minutes

Cooking time
45 minutes

Serves 4

Difficulty Medium

Ingredients

4 large potatoes
200g loin of pork, minced
70g bacon bits
2 tomatoes, skinned and seeded
½ onion, peeled and finely chopped
2 tablespoons raisins
1 tablespoon flaked almonds
2 sprigs parsley, chopped
salt and pepper

Preparation

Peel, rinse and dry the potatoes. Slice off the tops of the potatoes lengthways and set this aside. Scoop out the inside of the potatoes, taking care not to pierce the outer skin.

Put the pulp in a pan, cover with water, season with salt and cook for 15 minutes. Drain and mash.

Chop the tomatoes and cook over a gentle heat until reduced to a purée.

Fry the onion and bacon together until the onions are transparent.

Add the pork, almonds and raisins, and cook for 15 minutes.

Preheat oven to 180°C.

Transfer the tomato purée to an oven dish, arrange the empty potato cases on top, fill them with the meat mixture and then the mashed potato. Cover each with the slices set aside.

Sprinkle with parsley, drizzle a little oil and bake for 15 minutes.

Serve hot.

Mexico

Potato soup with cheese

Preparation time
15 minutes

Cooking time
50 minutes

Serves 4

Difficulty Easy

Ingredients

400g potatoes, diced

3 carrots, peeled and diced

2 onions, peeled and diced

200g feta

50g butter

bunch of chives, chopped

2 sprigs of parsley, chopped

1 litre chicken stock

1 teaspoon paprika

salt, pepper and cayenne pepper

Preparation

Melt the oil in a pan and fry the onions and carrots for 20 minutes over a gentle heat.

Add the potatoes, parsley, spices and chicken stock. Add salt, pepper and cayenne pepper to taste. Cook for a further 30 minutes.

Liquidise the soup in a blender and transfer to a soup tureen. Cut the feta into small cubes and add them to the soup, together with the chives.

Serve hot.

Moldova

Pyrjoale

Preparation time
25 minutes

Cooking time
30 minutes

Serves 4

Difficulty Easy

Ingredients

3 potatoes
500g veal
500g loin of pork
350g white bread, with crusts removed
2 onions, peeled and chopped
4 eggs, beaten
150ml milk
200g breadcrumbs
200g butter
½ bunch of dill, chopped
4 sprigs of parsley, chopped
salt and pepper

Preparation

Put the bread in the milk and leave it to soak.

Fry the onions in a knob of butter.

Mince the veal and pork, combine with the dill and parsley.

Peel and grate the potatoes.

In a large bowl mix together the meat, onions, potato, soaked bread which you have drained, herbs and eggs. Add 100g butter cut into small pieces, season with salt and pepper.

Form the mixture into balls, flatten each to make an oval pancake and roll them in the breadcrumbs.

Melt the rest of the butter in a large frying pan. Fry the pancakes until golden brown on both sides.

Serve hot.

Provençal tourtons

Preparation time
20 minutes

Cooking time
35 minutes

Serves 6

Difficulty Medium

Ingredients

1½ kg potatoes

3 leeks, trimmed, washed and cut into thin strips

1 onion, peeled and cut into thin strips

1 Saint-Marcellin, diced

4 tablespoons cream

100g grated gruyère

500g flour

125g butter

2 eggs

frying oil

salt and pepper

Preparation

Put the flour in a bowl, make a well in the centre and add the eggs, the butter cut into small pieces and a little salt. Knead together to obtain a smooth dough.

Peel the potatoes, cut them into pieces, steam or cook in boiling salted water for 20 minutes. Drain and mash.

Fry the leeks and onion in a knob of butter. When they are soft add them to the potatoes, together with the cream, gruyère, diced Saint-Marcellin, and a little salt and pepper. Knead together well.

Roll the dough out on a lightly floured surface. Using a cutter, cut out rounds. Spoon some potato stuffing onto half the rounds, cover with the remaining rounds and seal the edges by pinching them firmly.

Heat the oil in a pan and fry the tourtons for 5–10 minutes. Drain on kitchen paper and serve hot.

Monaco

Egypt, South Africa, Algeria and Morocco provide 80 per cent of Africa's production of potatoes. Thanks to irrigation systems, these countries have increased their growth rates by 5 per cent each year since the 1960s.

Lamb with potato

Preparation time
15 minutes

Cooking time
1 hour

Serves 4

Difficulty Easy

Ingredients

1 kg potatoes
1 kg shoulder of lamb, cut into pieces
3 carrots, peeled
1 litre milk
2 bay leaves
salt and pepper

Preparation

Put the lamb, bay leaves and carrots in a large pan, add the milk, season with salt and pepper and cook for 45 minutes.

Peel the potatoes, cut them into pieces, steam or cook in boiling salted water for 15 minutes.

Remove the meat from the pan and strain the liquid. Put the liquid back in the pan, together with the meat and potatoes. Continue cooking for 10 minutes.

Serve hot.

Maakouda

Preparation time
20 minutes

Cooking time
30 minutes

Serves 4

Difficulty Easy

Ingredients

1 kg potatoes
3 garlic cloves, peeled and chopped
4 eggs
3 tablespoons flour
1 teaspoon mild pimento
1 teaspoon ground cumin
a pinch of saffron strands
1 tablespoon olive oil
oil for deep frying
4 sprigs of fresh coriander, chopped
salt

Preparation

Steam or boil the unpeeled potatoes for 25 minutes, drain and set aside to cool completely.

Peel the potatoes. In a bowl, mash them, add the garlic, pimento, cumin, saffron, coriander, olive oil and a little salt. Beat the eggs, add to the mixture. Combine to form a smooth dough.

Heat the frying oil to 200°C. Put the flour into a bowl. Form small balls of dough, roll each one in flour and deep-fry until golden brown. Drain on kitchen paper.

Morocco

Potato tajine with onions and lemon

Preparation time
15 minutes

Cooking time
25 minutes

Serves 4

Difficulty Easy

Ingredients

800g potatoes
2 tablespoons black olives
2 onions, peeled and finely chopped
1g saffron strands
4 pinches of ground ginger
1 large crystallized lemon
4 tablespoons olive oil
100ml chicken stock

Morocco

Preparation

Peel the potatoes and cut into quarters.

Chop the crystallized lemon into small dice.

Heat the oil in a tajine dish, add the onion and cook for 5 minutes stirring all the time. Add the potatoes, lemon, saffron, ginger and stock. Combine well and leave to cook for 20 minutes. Add the olives just before serving.

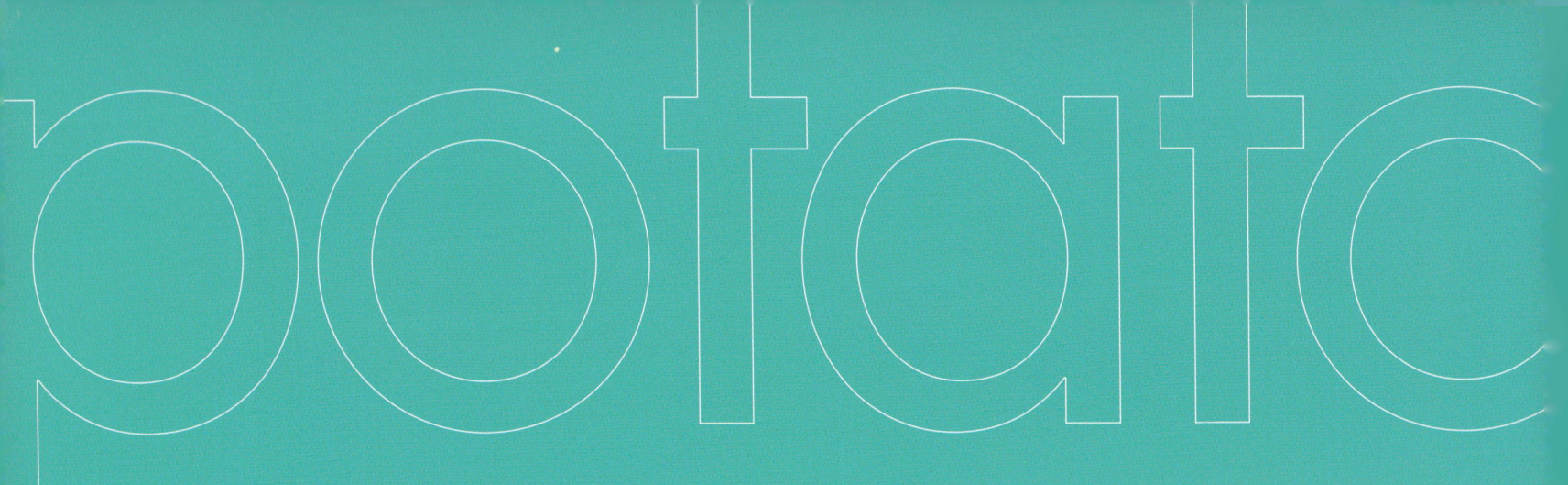

What are potatoes used for?

Not only used for eating and drinking, the potato is pulling off an uncommonly industrial career. When processed by the potato-starch industry, you find it returning in the form of dextrin, adhesives or starch in such food products as beverages and biscuits. It is also used by the pharmaceutical, textile, wood and paper industries. It has even penetrated into mineral oil drilling: starch derivatives are used during prewashing of boreholes.

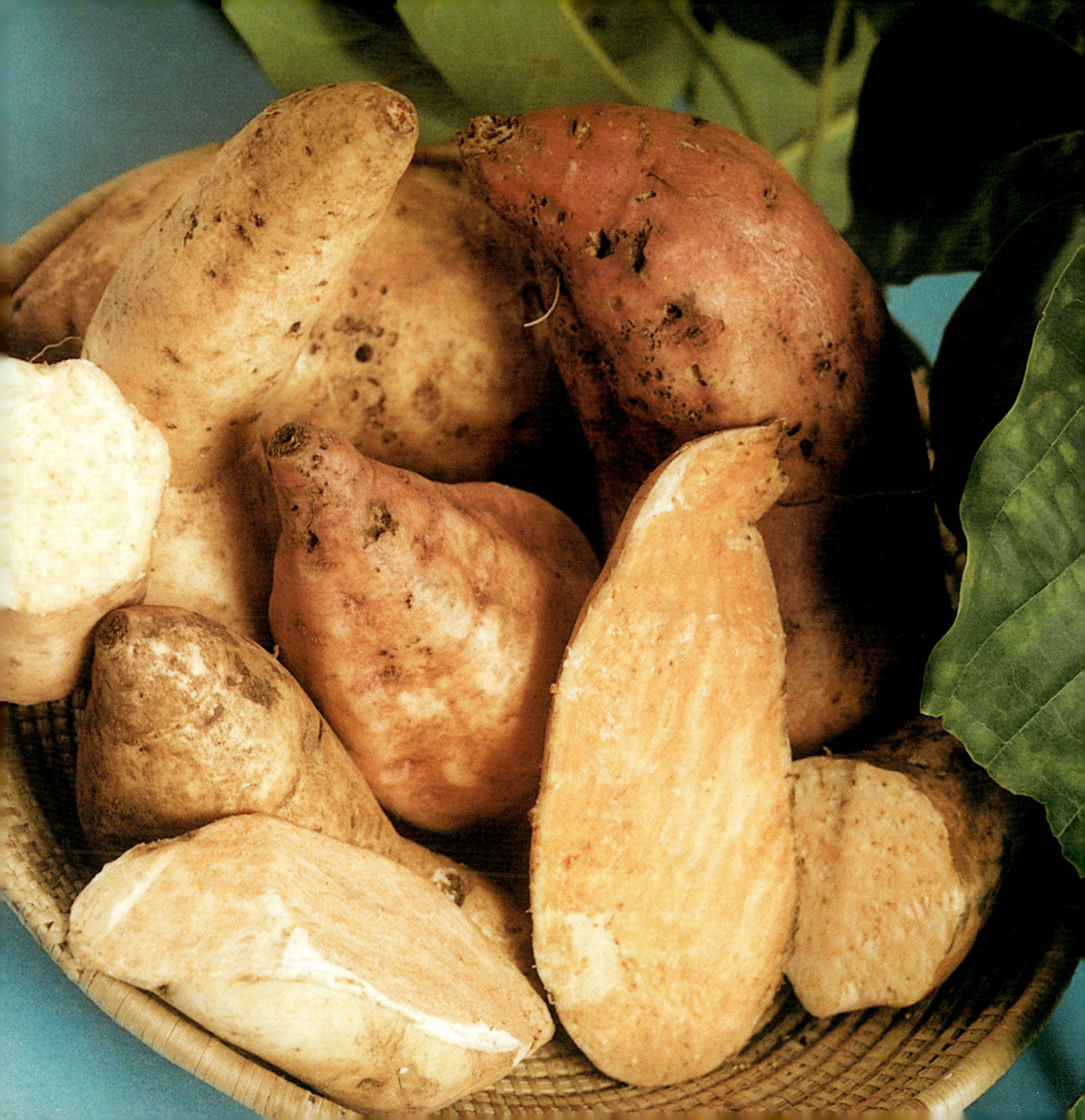

Potato with bacon

Preparation time
15 minutes

Cooking time
45 minutes

Serves 4

Difficulty Easy

Ingredients
1 kg potatoes
400g smoked bacon
300g sharp apples
300g mild apples
2 tablespoons molasses
salt and pepper

Netherlands

Preparation

Cook the bacon in a large pan of water for 25 minutes.

Peel the potatoes and apples. Cut them into small pieces and add to the pan. Simmer for 20 minutes, then drain.

Cut the bacon into thin slices. Mash together the potatoes and apples, season with salt and pepper, and stir in the molasses. Transfer to a serving dish and garnish with the bacon slices.

Serve hot.

Molasses are a by-product from the processing of sugarcane or sugar beet. Brown sugar melted in a little water can be used instead.

Stamppot boerenkool - (Kale hash)

Preparation time 15 minutes

Cooking time 35 minutes

Serves 4

Difficulty Easy

Ingredients
1 kg potatoes
1 kg kale, finely chopped
100ml milk
500g smoked sausage
80g butter
salt and pepper

Preparation

Peel and dice the potatoes.

Put the potatoes and kale in a large pan, cover with water, add salt, pepper and the smoked sausage. Bring to the boil, cover and simmer for 30 minutes.

Remove the sausage and cut it into slices. Mash vegetables with a fork, then incorporate the milk and butter. Transfer to a serving dish and garnish with slices of sausage.

Serve hot.

Netherlands

This typically Dutch dish provides a hearty meal.

Asaro

Preparation time
15 minutes

Cooking time
20 minutes

Serves 4

Difficulty Easy

Ingredients

800g potatoes

2 tomatoes, chopped

1 pepper, seeded and cut into fine strips

1 onion, peeled and chopped

200g fresh spinach, trimmed, washed and chopped

4 tablespoons tomato sauce

salt and pepper

Nigeria

Preparation

Peel and wash the potatoes, cut them into cubes.

Put the tomatoes, pepper and onion in a large pan, cover with water and season with salt and pepper.

Cook for 20 minutes, then add the spinach. Cook for a further 5 minutes.

Serve hot.

You can add meat, poultry meat or fish to this dish.

Baconbakte småpoteter

Preparation time
15 minutes

Cooking time
30 minutes

Serves 4

Difficulty Easy

Ingredients

12 small potatoes
12 slices of bacon
100g butter
3 tablespoons soy sauce
grated zest of 1 untreated lemon
2 tablespoons thyme

Preparation

Steam or boil the unpeeled potatoes for 25 minutes. Drain and peel them.

Wrap each potato in a slice of bacon and hold it in place with a toothpick.

Heat a knob of butter in a frying pan and cook the potatoes until golden brown. Transfer them to a serving dish.

Melt the butter in a pan, add the soy sauce, thyme and lemon zest.

Pour this sauce over the potatoes and serve hot.

Norway

Potatoes with salmon

Preparation time
20 minutes

Cooking time
60 minutes

Serves 4

Difficulty Easy

Ingredients

8 large new potatoes

400g fillet of Norwegian salmon

2 tablespoons thick fresh cream

3 sprigs of dill, chopped

1 egg yolk

salt and pepper

Preparation

Wrap each potato in aluminium foil and bake in the oven at 240°C for 30 to 40 minutes, depending on their size.

Poach the salmon in boiling salted water for 10 minutes, then drain.

Remove the tin foil from the potatoes, cut them in half lengthways and scoop out the centre, taking care not to piece the outer shell.

Flake the salmon into a bowl, add the potato pulp, salt and pepper, cream, egg yolk and dill. Combine thoroughly.

Fill the potato cases with the mixture. Arrange them in an oven dish and reheat for 5 minutes.

This dish can also be prepared using cod, haddock, or even chicken or ham.

Salmon and potato pudding

Preparation time
20 minutes

Cooking time
45 minutes

Serves 4

Difficulty Easy

Ingredients

800g potatoes
1 onion, peeled and chopped
400g smoked salmon, diced
2 eggs
2 tablespoons liquid cream
2 tablespoons sunflower oil
5 sprigs of dill, chopped
salt and pepper

Preparation

Peel the potatoes, steam or cook in boiling salted water for 25 minutes. Drain and mash.

Heat the oil in a pan and fry the onion.

Beat the eggs with the cream and a little salt and pepper.

Put the mash in a bowl and add the onions, eggs, dill and salmon.

Preheat the oven to 180°C.

Line some ramekins with greaseproof paper and spoon the mixture into them. Bake in the oven for 20 minutes. Let them get cold before tipping them out of the moulds.

Norway

potato

Are potatoes fattening?

No. A medium-sized potato provides 84 calories. Potatoes are thus comparable to a good number of fish and crustaceans (ray: 89 cal., shrimps: 96 cal.), to certain vegetables (salsifies: 76 cal., peas: 91 cal.) and to fruits (grape: 77 cal., banana: 94 cal.), foods that are preferable for composing light meals.

Potato skin contains a lot of fibre, and 80 per cent of the potato's weight is water.

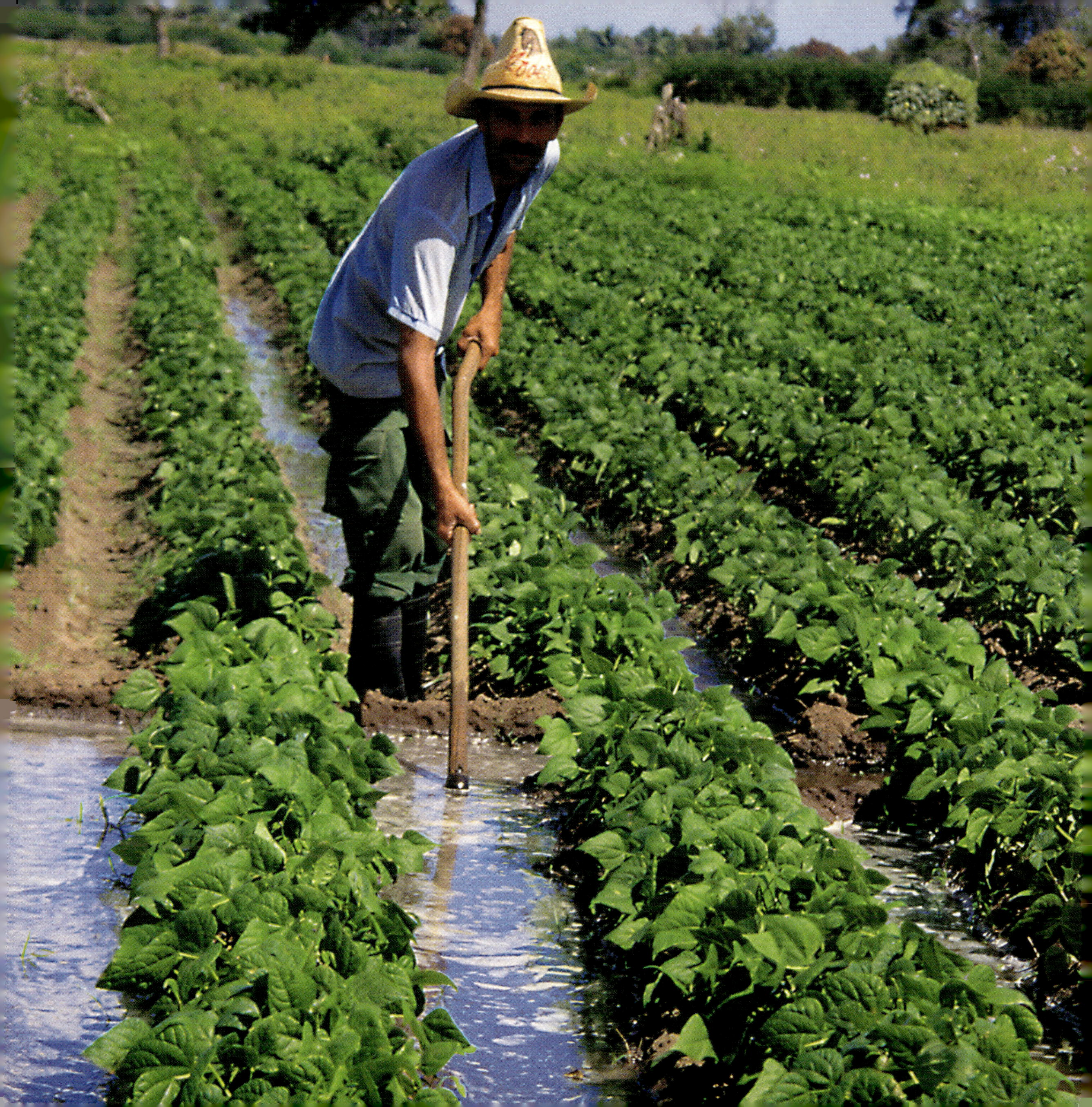

Vegetable biryani

Preparation time
15 minutes

Cooking time
50 minutes

Serves 6

Difficulty Easy

Ingredients

6 potatoes
3 carrots
150g cooked beans
4 spring onions, chopped
250g perfumed rice
3 garlic cloves, peeled and chopped
3cm piece of root ginger, peeled and grated
pinch of curcuma
2 pinches of ground pimento
½ bunch of coriander, chopped
½ bunch of mint, chopped
2 plain yoghurts
40g raisins
50g blanched almonds
50g butter
50g cashew nuts
salt

Preparation

Cook the rice in boiling salted water for 10 minutes, then drain.

Melt the butter in a frying pan and fry the onions, garlic, ginger, curcuma and pimento.

Peel the carrots and potatoes and dice them. Add them to the pan together with 150ml water. Cover and cook over a gentle heat for 10 minutes. Then add the beans and cook for a further 5 minutes.

Combine the coriander and mint with the yoghurt.

Transfer the vegetables to a large serving dish, add the rice and the raisins, almonds and cashew nuts.

Serve with the yoghurt sauce.

Naquis de batata

Preparation time
15 minutes

Cooking time
40 minutes

Serves 4

Difficulty Medium

Ingredients

500g sweet potatoes
750g flour
200g butter
salt

Preparation

Peel the sweet potatoes, cook in boiling salted water for 30 minutes. Drain and mash.

Mix the mash with the flour to obtain a smooth dough.

Form the dough into small sausages

Bring a pan of salted water to the boil. Poach the sweet potatoes until they rise to the surface. Drain on kitchen paper and transfer to a serving dish.

Melt the butter and pour it over the sweet potatoes.

Paraguay

In 1778-1779 Prussia and Austria fought the War of the Bavarian Succession, but there was little fighting because each side was concerned with cutting its opponent's communications and denying it supplies. Contemporaries nicknamed the war the "potato war" (Kartoffelkrieg).

Cau cau

Preparation time
20 minutes

Cooking time
50 minutes

Serves 4

Difficulty Easy

Ingredients

1 kg potatoes
1 onion, peeled and chopped
500g tripe, washed and prepared
4 teaspoons ground pimento
1 teaspoon curcuma
1 teaspoon ground cumin
2 garlic cloves, peeled and chopped
2 sprigs of mint
salt and pepper

Peru

Preparation

Peel the potatoes and cut into cubes. Steam or cook in boiling salted water for 20 minutes, then drain.

Cut the tripe into dice. Bring a pan of salted water to the boil, add a sprig of mint and cook the tripe for 15 minutes.

In a large pan, fry the onion and garlic with a tablespoon of oil. Add the spices, salt and pepper. Add the tripe and potatoes, together with the sprigs of mint. Cook for 10 minutes.

Serve hot.

Ocopa

Preparation time
15 minutes

Cooking time
25 minutes

Serves 4

Difficulty Easy

Ingredients

800g potatoes
150g fromage frais
2 small chillies
4 tablespoons chopped walnuts
6 tablespoons oil
a few lettuce leaves
salt and pepper

Preparation

Peel and wash the potatoes. Cut them into pieces, steam or cook in boiling salted water for 25 minutes, then drain them.

Remove the seeds from the chillies and chop them.

Mix the cheese with the chillies, chopped walnuts, the oil and a little salt and pepper.

Arrange the lettuce leaves on a serving dish, add the potatoes and spoon the sauce on top.

Peru

Papas à la huancaina

Preparation time
15 minutes

Cooking time
50 minutes

Serves 4

Difficulty Easy

Ingredients

1 kg potatoes
400g fromage blanc
4 bitter oranges
1 teaspoon ground pimento
4 eggs
4 lettuce leaves
salt

Peru

Preparation

Boil the eggs for about 10 minutes until they are hard-boiled. Run them under cold water and shell them. Put them aside.

Peel and rinse the potatoes and cut into pieces.

Squeeze the oranges and pour the juice into a pan. Add the fromage blanc and pimento, season with salt and stir together.

Add the potatoes to this sauce and cook over a gentle heat for about 30 minutes.

Wrap each hard-boiled egg in a lettuce leaf and arrange on separate plates. Garnish with the potato mixture.

Vary the quantity of pimento to suit your own taste.

Papas rellenas

Preparation time
25 minutes

Cooking time
50 minutes

Serves 4

Difficulty Medium

Ingredients

1 kg potatoes
250g minced meat
4 tablespoons flour
2 eggs, beaten separately
3 hard-boiled eggs, sliced
1 onion, peeled and chopped
2 garlic cloves, peeled and chopped
100g raisins
3 olives, chopped
2 tablespoons olive oil
oil for deep frying
salt and pepper

Preparation

Steam or boil the unpeeled potatoes for 25 minutes. Peel and mash them. Add a little salt and one of the beaten eggs.

Fry the onion and garlic in 2 tablespoons of oil for 2 minutes. Add the minced meat and fry for 10 minutes. Add the olives and raisins.

On a lightly floured surface roll the mashed potato into a long sausage. Divide it into 12 and form each one into a nest. Put a slice of hard-boiled egg and some meat mixture into each nest. Close the potato over the meat.

Put the flour in one shallow dish and the other beaten egg in another. Dip each potato nest into the egg, then roll them in the flour.

Heat the frying oil and fry the potato nests until golden brown.

Drain on kitchen paper and serve hot.

Peru

Serve these papas with a criolla sauce made of chopped onion, garlic and chilli, mixed with lemon juice, vinegar and oil.

Adobong gulay

Preparation time
15 minutes

Cooking time
35 minutes

Serves 4

Difficulty Easy

Ingredients

600g potatoes
1 onion, peeled and chopped
3 garlic cloves, peeled and chopped
2 bay leaves
1 teaspoon peppercorns
4 tablespoons vegetable oil
1 teaspoon soy sauce
1 teaspoon vinegar
salt and pepper
sugar

Philippines

Preparation

Heat the oil in a pan, add the peppercorns and bay leaves and fry for 2 minutes.

Add the garlic and onion and cook for 5 minutes, stirring all the time. Add a little sugar, salt and pepper, the vinegar and soy sauce.

Peel the potatoes; cut them into quarters and add them to the pan. Mix well and cook over a gentle heat for 25 minutes.

Kluski slaskie

Preparation time
20 minutes

Cooking time
15 minutes

Serves 4

Difficulty Medium

Ingredients
800g potatoes
60g potato flour
salt

Preparation

Peel the potatoes, steam or boil them for 25 minutes.

Drain and mash them.

Add a little salt and the potato flour. Set aside to cool.

When cool, form the mixture into nut-sized balls.

Bring a pan of salted water to the boil and poach the potato balls. When they rise to the surface remove them with a slotted spoon. Drain on kitchen paper.

Serve hot.

According to Polish tradition, a hole should be made in each potato ball before poaching – a sort of trademark.

Poland

Placki de Czesiu

Preparation time
20 minutes

Cooking time
30 minutes

Serves 6

Difficulty Easy

Ingredients

2 kg potatoes
2 onions, peeled and finely chopped
1 shallot, peeled and finely chopped
1 garlic clove, peeled and finely chopped
3 eggs, beaten
6 sprigs of parsley, chopped
3 tablespoons flour
100g butter
salt and pepper

Preparation

Peel and grate the potatoes. Combine them with the onions, garlic, shallot and parsley.

Add the eggs and season with salt and pepper. Stir in the flour, mixing thoroughly to form a dough.

Divide the dough into 6 and form each into a thick pattie.

Melt the butter in a large frying pan. Fry the patties on one side until golden brown. Turn them over and cook the other side until golden brown, adding more butter if necessary. Drain on kitchen paper before serving.

This dish is a good accompaniment for meat, or can even be eaten as a dessert, sprinkled with sugar.

Pyzy z mięsem

Preparation time
30 minutes

Cooking time
35 minutes

Serves 4

Difficulty Medium

Ingredients

1 kg potatoes
1 whole egg, beaten
1 egg yolk
8 tablespoons flour
300g cooked meat (pork or beef), chopped
2 slices of bread, crumbled
1 onion, chopped
2 tablespoons oil
100g smoked bacon bits
parsley, chopped
salt, pepper and koperek

Preparation

Peel and wash the potatoes. Steam or cook half the potatoes in boiling salted water for 25 minutes, drain and mash. Grate the rest of the uncooked potatoes.

Combine the meat, onion and bread. Add the whole beaten egg, parsley, season with salt and pepper. Mix together thoroughly and add a little flour to thicken.

Form the mixture into small balls. Poach them in boiling salted water. Arrange them in a serving dish and garnish with koperek.

Serve hot.

Poland

Koperek is a typically Polish spice which resembles dill. It can be found in specialist grocery stores.

Cod and shrimp gratin

Preparation time
30 minutes

Cooking time
55 minutes

Serves 4

Difficulty Easy

Ingredients

800g potatoes
400ml milk
400g unsalted cod
400g shrimps
2 tomatoes
1 onion, peeled and chopped
2 garlic cloves, chopped
200ml cream
100ml olive oil
4 sprigs of parsley
2 tablespoons breadcrumbs
salt, pepper, nutmeg

Portugal

Preparation

Peel and dry the potatoes. Cut them into pieces, steam or cook in boiling salted water for 20 minutes. Drain and mash them. Add the milk, season with salt, pepper and a little nutmeg.

Poach the cod. Drain, remove the bones and flake.

Peel the shrimps. Peel the tomatoes, remove the seeds and chop.

Fry the onion and garlic in a tablespoon of oil. Add the tomatoes and cook for 10 minutes.

Preheat the oven to 180°C.

Layer half the potatoes in an oven dish, cover with the cod, shrimps and vegetables, parsley and then the rest of the potatoes. Sprinkle with breadcrumbs and drizzle with a little olive oil.

Bake in the oven for 15 minutes.

Serve hot.

Potatoes with cabbage

Preparation time
10 minutes

Cooking time
60 minutes

Serves 4

Difficulty Easy

Ingredients

500g potatoes
1 cabbage, cut into fine strips
2 garlic cloves
2 tablespoons olive oil
2 slices of bread
salt and pepper

Preparation

Peel the potatoes and cut into pieces.

Place the cabbage and potatoes in a large pan, add the oil, garlic and bread, season with salt and pepper and add enough water so that the vegetables are just covered.

Cover and bring to the boil, lower the heat and simmer for an hour.

Beat the vegetables with a fork until they form a thick purée.

Serve hot.

Portugal

Potatoes with garlic cream

Preparation time
20 minutes

Cooking time
20 minutes

Serves 4

Difficulty Easy

Ingredients
1 kg potatoes
4 tablespoons paprika
2 garlic cloves, crushed
1 bay leaf, finely chopped
4 tablespoons olive oil
salt and pepper

Portugal

Preparation

Wash and dry the potatoes.

Put the garlic, paprika, salt, pepper, bay leaf and oil in a bowl, combine thoroughly to form a purée.

Make deep cuts in each potato and insert some of the purée into each cut. Set aside for 2 hours.

Arrange the potatoes in an oven dish and cook for about 20 minutes at 180°C.

Choose potatoes of about the same size.

potato

Who painted the *Potato Eaters* at the beginning of his career in 1885?

Vincent van Gogh was the first to recognize the potato in the world of the fine arts. He saw the potato as the symbol of man's relationship with the soil, of the labour that must be produced to earn his food, to subsist and to continue to live.

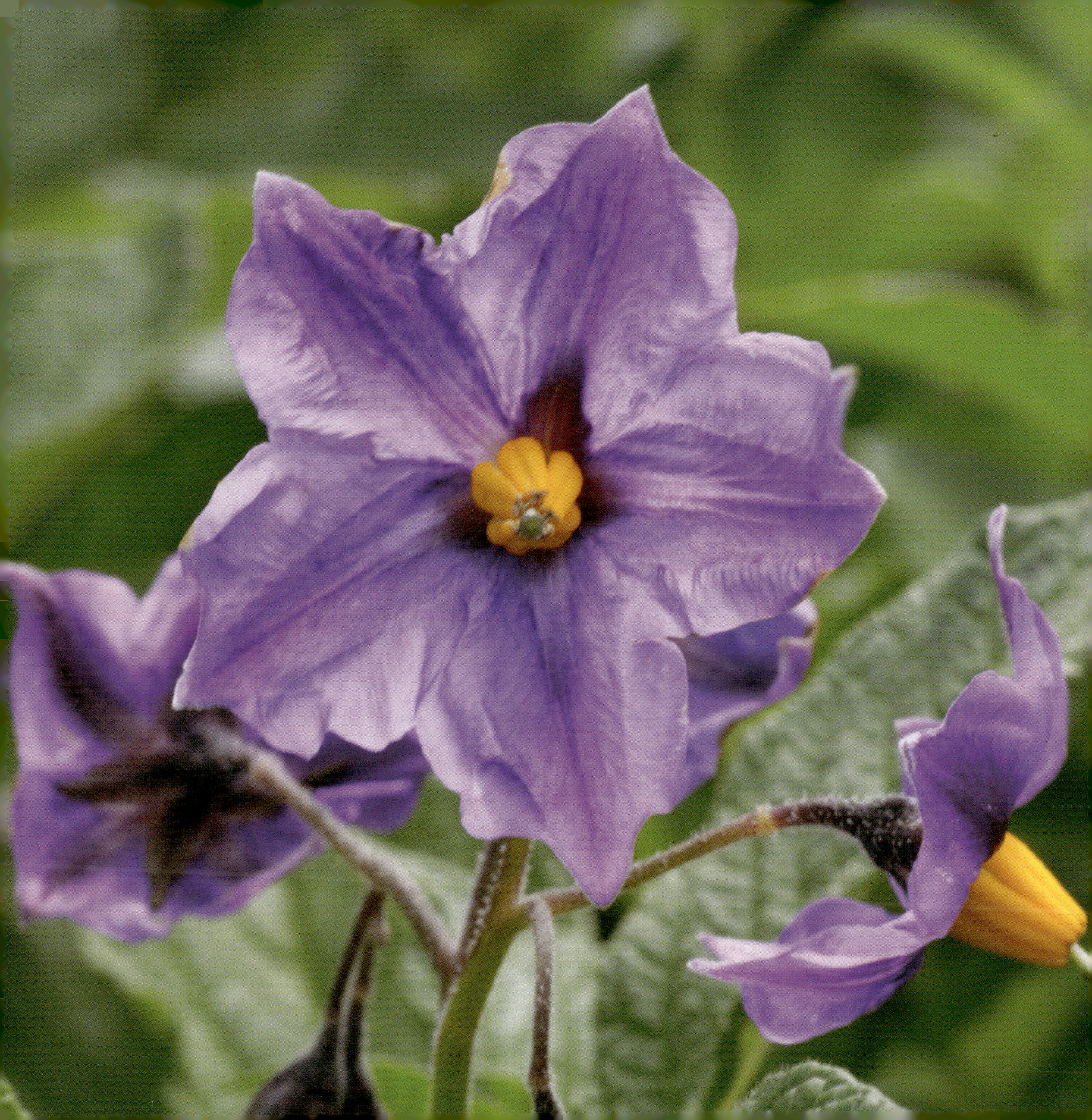

Korean potatoes

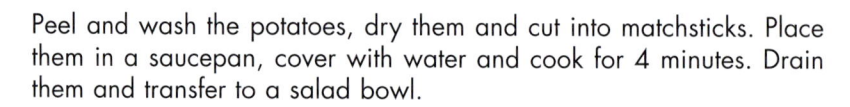

Preparation time
10 minutes

Cooking time
4 minutes

Serves 4

Difficulty Easy

Ingredients

600g potatoes
3 garlic cloves, peeled and crushed
2 tablespoons sugar
2 tablespoons soy sauce
2 tablespoons sesame seeds
2 tablespoons sesame oil

Preparation

Peel and wash the potatoes, dry them and cut into matchsticks. Place them in a saucepan, cover with water and cook for 4 minutes. Drain them and transfer to a salad bowl.

Mix together the garlic, soy sauce, sugar, sesame oil and sesame seeds. Pour the sauce over the potatoes and stir gently.

Republic of Korea

Fossilized remains of possibly cultivated tubers found on a cave floor in Chilca Canyon suggest that the potato was cultivated at least from about 7,000 years ago.

Potato and ham fritters

Preparation time
30 minutes

Cooking time
45 minutes

Serves 4

Difficulty Medium

Ingredients

800g potatoes
1 thick slice of ham, chopped
250g flour
3 egg yolks
10g baker's yeast
100ml milk, warmed
oil for deep-frying
salt

Preparation

Steam or boil the unpeeled potatoes for 25 minutes, peel and mash them.

Dissolve the yeast in the milk.

Put the flour in a large bowl. Make a well in the centre, add a pinch of salt, the yeast and the egg yolks. Knead them together to obtain a smooth dough.

Add the mashed potatoes and mix thoroughly.

Divide the dough in two and roll out each half separately on a lightly floured surface. Cut out rounds using a cutter. Spoon the ham into the centre of half the rounds, cover with the other half and seal the edges by pinching firmly.

Cover with a cloth and set aside in a warm place for 1 hour.

Fry in hot oil until golden brown.

Romania

Vegetable moussaka

Preparation time
30 minutes

Cooking time
50 minutes

Serves 4

Difficulty Easy

Ingredients

1 kg potatoes
3 onions, peeled and chopped
1 kg aubergines
1 kg tomatoes
1 pepper
bunch of parsley, chopped
bunch of dill, chopped
6 tablespoons breadcrumbs
7 tablespoons olive oil
salt and pepper

Romania

Preparation

Chop the aubergine into small dice. Do the same with the tomatoes, leaving 2 whole.

Peel the potatoes and cut into sticks. Remove the seeds from the pepper and cut it into small dice. Combine the onions with the parsley and dill.

Heat 2 tablespoons of oil in a frying pan, add the onions, parsley, dill, aubergines, pepper and chopped tomatoes. Season with salt and pepper.

Heat 2 tablespoons oil in a pan and fry the potatoes for 5 minutes

Preheat the oven to 180°C.

Grease a gratin dish, arrange in it a layer of potatoes, followed by a layer of vegetables, and continue in layers, ending with potatoes. Cut the remaining 2 tomatoes into slices and lay them on top of the potatoes. Sprinkle with breadcrumbs and drizzle oil over the top.

Bake in the oven for 30 minutes.

Serve hot.

This dish is served during Lent.

Piroshki

Preparation time 30 minutes

Cooking time 30 minutes

Serves 4

Difficulty Medium

Ingredients

For the dough:
800g flour
1 tablespoon dry yeast
1 egg + 2 egg yolks
500ml milk
250g butter
50g sugar

For the stuffing:
250g potatoes
400g minced beef
4 thin slices bacon
1 onion, peeled and chopped
1 garlic clove, peeled and chopped
100g tomato concentrate
2 teaspoons thyme
1 tablespoon olive oil
salt and pepper

Preparation

To make the dough: In a large bowl mix together the flour, yeast, sugar, and a tablespoon of salt. Make a well in the centre and add the egg yolks, milk and butter. Knead the dough until it forms a ball and does not stick to the bowl. Cover the bowl with a cloth. Set in a warm place and allow to rise until doubled in volume.

Peel and rinse the potatoes, dry and grate them with a fine grater. Put in a bowl with the onion, garlic, bacon, minced beef, thyme, tomato concentrate, season with salt and pepper and combine thoroughly.

Heat the oil in a pan and fry the stuffing for 15 minutes.

Set aside to cool.

Preheat the oven to 180°C and oil 2 baking trays.

Knead the dough on a lightly floured surface until it is elastic. Divide it into 16 pieces. Roll each piece into a ball and then flatten to form disks about 12cm in diameter.

Spoon some stuffing onto each disk, fold the disks over and pinch the edges firmly to seal.

Beat the whole egg and brush the top of each piroshki. Arrange them on the baking trays. Set aside in a warm place for 15 minutes.

Bake for 15 minutes.

Serve hot or warm.

These piroshki are served as a starter.

Russian Federation

Selyodka pod shouboy (Herring under a fur coat)

Russian Federation

Preparation time
20 minutes

Cooking time
25 minutes

Serves 4

Difficulty Easy

Ingredients

6 potatoes
4 cooked beetroot, grated
8 carrots, peeled and grated
4 hard-boiled eggs, chopped
1 packet of herring (vacuum-packed), diced
4 tablespoons liquid cream
125g mayonnaise
salt

Preparation

Peel the potatoes, steam or cook them in boiling salted water for 25 minutes. Drain them and cut into thin slices.

Combine the beetroot with half the mayonnaise and cream, mix the remaining mayonnaise and cream with the carrots.

In a serving dish arrange the ingredients in layers as follows: herring, carrots, eggs, beetroot, potatoes, carrots, herring, eggs, and ending with beetroot.

Stuffed potatoes

Preparation time
30 minutes

Cooking time
1 hour 10 minutes

Serves 4

Difficulty Easy

Ingredients

8 medium-sized potatoes
750g minced beef
1 onion, peeled and chopped
2 garlic cloves, peeled and chopped
90ml oil
300ml sour cream
500ml tomato sauce
salt and pepper

Preparation

Peel the potatoes and scoop out the pulp, taking care not to pierce the outer shell.

Fry the onion in a little oil. Remove from the heat and add the tomato sauce and sour cream.

In a bowl combine the meat, garlic, salt and pepper. Add the onion sauce and mix thoroughly.

Preheat the oven to 180°C.

Spoon the mixture into the potato cases. Arrange them in a gratin dish and drizzle with the remaining oil.

Bake in the oven for an hour.

Serve hot.

Russian Federation

Vegetable borsch

Russian Federation

Preparation time
20 minutes

Cooking time
45 minutes

Serves 4

Difficulty Easy

Ingredients

6 potatoes

1 raw beetroot, skinned and cut into thin sticks

1 large white cabbage, chopped finely

2 carrots, peeled and sliced

1 onion, peeled and chopped

2 sprigs of dill

2 sprigs of parsley

1 bay leaf

salt and pepper

Preparation

Peel, wash and dice the potatoes. Steam or cook them in boiling salted water for 20 minutes.

Heat the oil in a pan and fry the onions, cabbage and carrots for 3 minutes.

Drain the potatoes, keeping the cooking liquid. Add to this liquid the beetroot, cabbage, carrots and onion. Add the bay leaf, parsley and dill. Bring to the boil and simmer for 20 minutes. Put the potatoes back in the pan and continue cooking for 5 minutes.

Serve hot.

This borsch made without meat is served during Lent.

potato

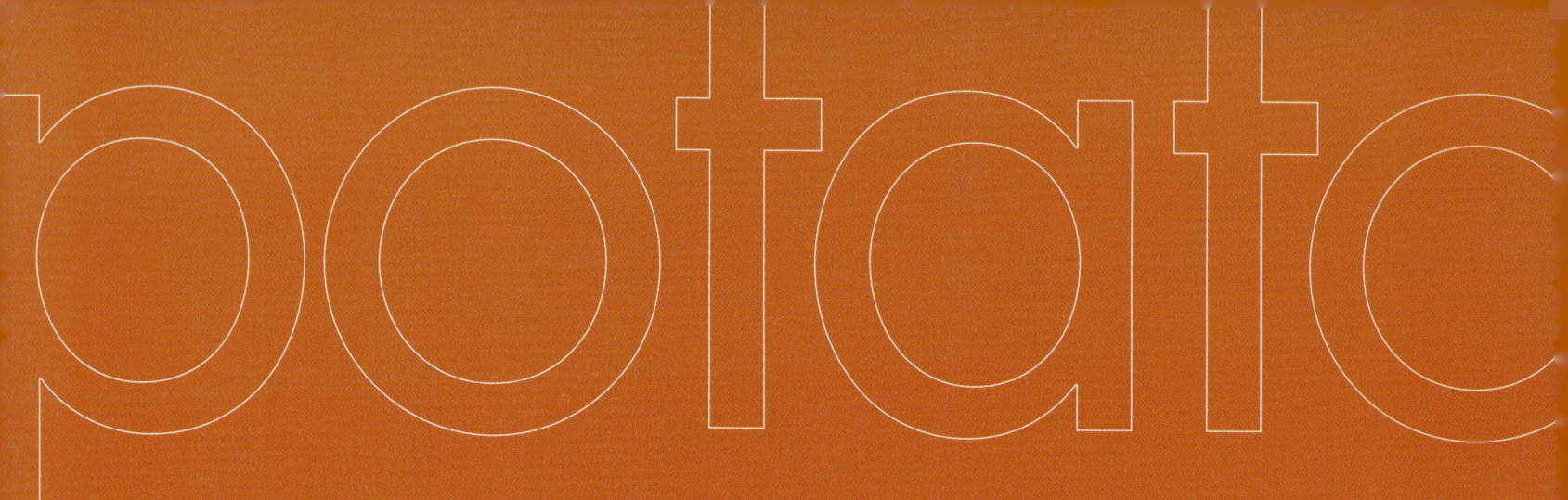

When was the potato chip invented?

The potato chip was allegedly invented in 1853 in Saratoga Springs, New York. To take revenge on a difficult customer who repeatedly complained about his thick fried potatoes, the young cook George Crum defiantly prepared a handful of superthin potato slices, plunged them into the deep fryer and served them to the customer, who loved them.

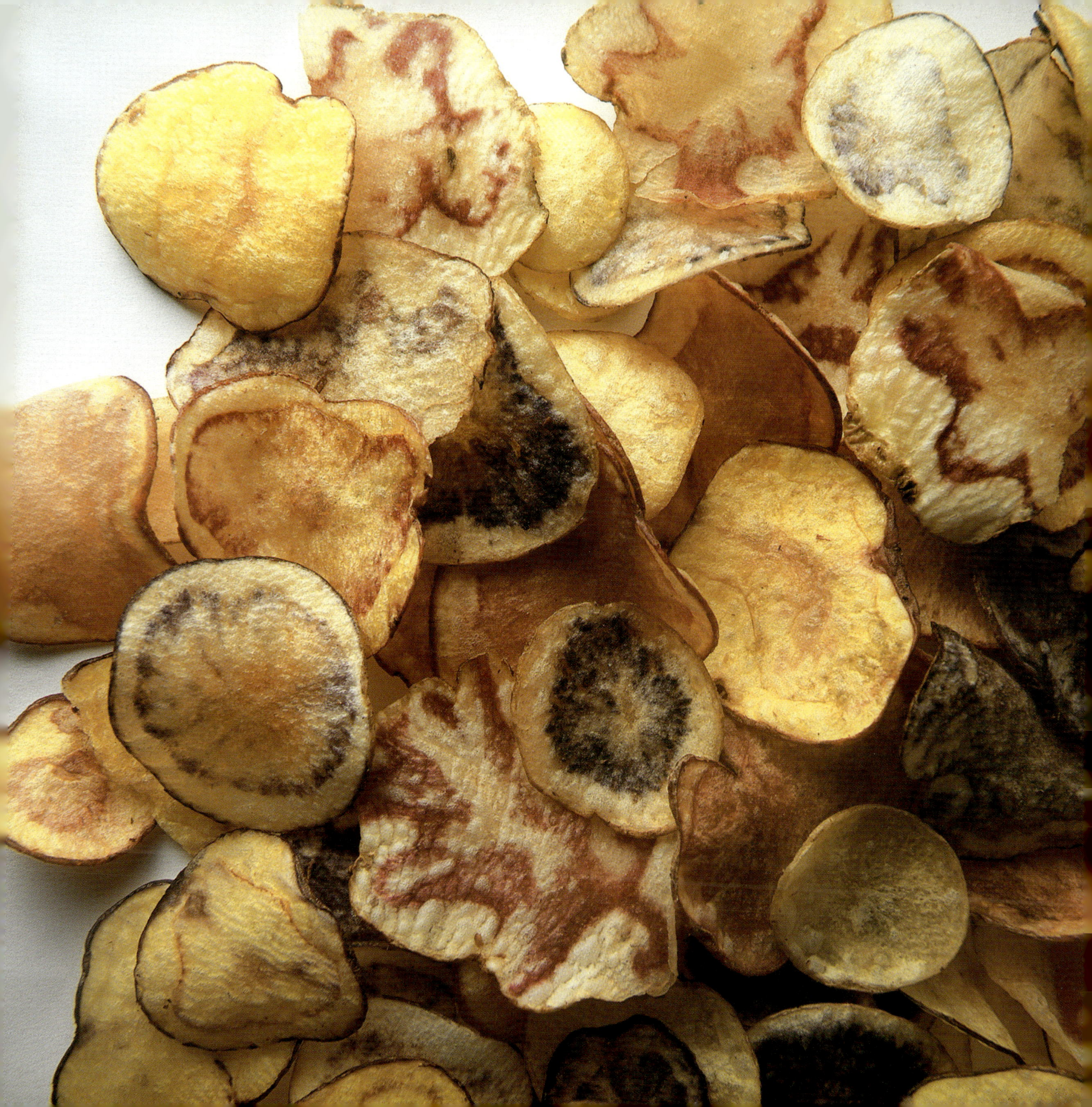

Sweet potato jam

Preparation time
10 minutes

Cooking time
50 minutes

Serves 6

Difficulty Easy

Ingredients

1 kg sweet potatoes

800g sugar

zest of an untreated lemon

1 teaspoon grated ginger

1 pinch grated nutmeg

Senegal

Preparation

Put the sugar into a pan, add 2 litres of water, the lemon zest, ginger and nutmeg. Cook for 20 minutes to form a syrup.

Peel and wash the sweet potatoes, cut them into cubes. Cook in boiling water for 10 minutes, then drain them well.

Add the potatoes to the syrup and continue cooking for 25 minutes.

Sterilise some pots with boiling water, pour the hot jam into them and seal them tightly.

Potato pita

Preparation time
15 minutes

Cooking time
30 minutes

Serves 4

Difficulty Medium

Ingredients

1 kg potatoes
2 onions, peeled and chopped
100ml oil
salt and pepper
8 sheets of brick dough or filo pastry

Preparation

Peel and wash the potatoes, dry them thoroughly and grate them.

Fry the onions gently in 2 tablespoons of oil until coloured.

Add the potatoes, season with salt and pepper and cook for 15 minutes, stirring often.

Place a sheet of brick dough or filo pastry on a work surface, spoon some of the mixture into the middle, then roll up the sheet and tuck in the ends to form a small packet. Continue like this with the other sheets.

Arrange the pita on a greased oven tray. Brush with oil and bake in the oven at 210°C for about 10 minutes until golden brown.

Serve hot or warm.

Serbia

Put the sheets of brick dough on a damp cloth before filling them – this stops them from breaking.

Bramboraky

Slovakia

Preparation time
20 minutes

Cooking time
15 minutes

Serves 6

Difficulty Easy

Ingredients

2½ kg potatoes
1 onion, peeled and chopped
230g fine semolina
1 egg
1 garlic clove, peeled and chopped
2 tablespoons oil
salt and pepper

Preparation

Peel the potatoes and grate them with a fine grater. Put in a colander and let them drain and release their liquid for 30 minutes.

Put the potatoes in a bowl, add the onion, garlic, egg, semolina, salt and pepper, and combine thoroughly. Spread the mixture out on a lightly floured surface and cut out pancakes of about 12cm in diameter.

Heat the oil in a large pan and fry the pancakes on one side until golden brown. Turn them over and cook the other side until golden brown.

Serve these potato pancakes with sauerkraut.

Halusky

Preparation time
20 minutes

Cooking time
10 minutes

Serves 6

Difficulty Medium

Ingredients
1 kg potatoes
200g flour
2 eggs
250g sheep's cheese
4 tablespoons milk
4 tablespoons oil
salt

Preparation

Peel and grate the potatoes. Place them in a bowl and add the milk, eggs, flour and a little salt. Combine the ingredients and knead to form a smooth dough.

Roll the dough into a long sausage shape. Cut into thin rounds.

Fill a large pan with salted water and bring to the boil. Drop the rounds of dough into the boiling water. As soon as they rise to the surface, count 5 minutes cooking time. Remove with a slotted spoon and drain on a cloth.

Arrange the rounds in a serving dish, crumble the sheep's cheese on top and sprinkle with oil.

Slovakia

Serve with fried bacon bits.

Potato terrine with cèpes

Preparation time
15 minutes

Cooking time
40 minutes

Serves 4

Difficulty Easy

Ingredients

8 long potatoes
150g cèpes
2 garlic cloves, peeled and chopped
2 tablespoons oil
40g butter
2 teaspoons thyme
2 sprigs flat leaf parsley, chopped
salt and pepper

Slovakia

Preparation

Peel, wash and dry the potatoes. Cut them into thin slices.

Wash and dry the cèpes, chop them finely and fry for 3 minutes in a tablespoon of oil and half the butter. Add the garlic, thyme and parsley, season with salt and pepper.

Preheat the oven to 180°C.

Line a small oven dish with greaseproof paper. Put a layer of potato on the bottom, overlapping the slices and lining also the sides of the dish. Add a layer of cèpes, and repeat with the rest of the ingredients, ending with a layer of potatoes.

Dot the top with butter and bake in the oven for 30 minutes.

Serve hot or warm.

Frika

Preparation time
15 minutes

Cooking time
25 minutes

Serves 4

Difficulty Easy

Ingredients
800g potatoes
320g grated cheese
6 tablespoons oil
salt and pepper

Preparation

Peel, wash and dry the potatoes, cut them into slices.

Heat the oil in a large pan, fry the potatoes for about 20 minutes, stirring often, until golden brown. Season with salt and pepper.

Sprinkle with the grated cheese, mix it in well and flatten the mixture to form a large pancake. Fry until the underside is golden brown, then turn it over carefully and brown the other side.

Slovenia

In Slovenia this dish is served with polenta.

Potato salad with eggs

Preparation time
20 minutes

Cooking time
25 minutes

Serves 4

Difficulty Easy

Ingredients

12 small potatoes

8 hard-boiled eggs, peeled and sliced

1 bunch of spring onions, peeled and finely chopped

150g sweet condensed milk

200g mayonnaise

4 sprigs of flat leaf parsley, chopped

Preparation

Steam or boil the unpeeled potatoes for 25 minutes, drain and leave to cool.

Combine the mayonnaise and condensed milk in a large salad bowl. Add the potatoes, onions and chopped parsley. Add the egg slices and stir carefully.

Serve cold.

South Africa

Potato stew

Preparation time
20 minutes

Cooking time
20 minutes

Serves 4

Difficulty Easy

Ingredients

4 potatoes
2 sweet potatoes
2 tablespoons olive oil
½ cauliflower, separated into small sprigs
2 onions, peeled and finely chopped
1 garlic clove, peeled and finely chopped
3cm piece of root ginger, peeled and finely chopped
2 teaspoons poppy seeds
1 teaspoon mustard seeds
1 tablespoon coriander seeds
4 whole cloves
1 tablespoon cider vinegar
2 tablespoons raisins
salt and freshly ground pepper

Preparation

Peel the potatoes and sweet potatoes, cut them into cubes.

Heat the oil in a frying pan, fry the garlic and the onion for 5 minutes, stirring all the time.

Add the ginger, poppy seeds, mustard seeds, coriander and cloves. Mix together, then add the potatoes.

Add 200ml water, season with salt and pepper. Bring to the boil, then lower the heat and leave it to cook uncovered for 5 minutes, stirring all the time.

Add the cauliflower, sweet potatoes and raisins. Cook for another 10 minutes.

Check that the vegetables are tender and cook a little longer if necessary.

Transfer to a serving dish and drizzle with cider vinegar.

This dish is traditionally prepared during the Kwanzaa festival, a week-long pan-African festival which takes place from 26 December to 1 January.

South Africa

Aïoli potatoes

Preparation time
15 minutes

Cooking time
20 minutes

Serves 4

Difficulty Easy

Ingredients

1 kg potatoes
2 egg yolks
2 garlic cloves, crushed
8 tablespoons olive oil
2 stalks parsley, chopped
salt and pepper

Spain

Preparation

Steam or boil the unpeeled potatoes for 20 minutes, peel them and cut them into thick slices. Transfer to a serving dish.

Place the garlic, egg yolks, salt and pepper in a bowl. Beat together and add the oil drop by drop, beating all the time

Pour the sauce over the potatoes.

Sprinkle with parsley just before serving.

Cocido

Preparation time
20 minutes

Cooking time
2 hours

Serves 4

Difficulty Easy

Ingredients

500g potatoes
250g chickpeas, soaked overnight in cold water
400g pumpkin, chopped
1 garlic clove, crushed
500g beef
100g bacon
100g smoked ham
2 hot chorizos
salt

Preparation

Put the beef, bacon, ham and chickpeas in a large pot and cover with cold water. Bring to the boil and simmer for 1½ hours.

Peel the potatoes, add to the pan together with the garlic, pumpkin, chorizos and a little salt. Continue cooking for 30 minutes.

Serve hot.

Cocido is a traditional Spanish dish.

Spain

Patatas bravas

Preparation time
20 minutes

Cooking time
40 minutes

Serves 4

Difficulty Easy

Ingredients

500g potatoes
150ml olive oil

For the sauce:
3 tomatoes, skinned and seeded
4 tablespoons olive oil
1 teaspoon white vinegar
1 onion
1 garlic clove, peeled and chopped
ground cayenne pepper
12 blanched almonds
10 blanched hazelnuts
1 slice brown bread
½ teaspoon mild paprika
salt

Spain

Preparation

To prepare the sauce: Toast the bread. Dry fry (without oil or fat) the garlic with the hazelnuts and almonds. In a food processor blend the tomatoes, garlic, onion, hazelnuts, almonds, 2 pinches of cayenne pepper, paprika, toasted bread, vinegar and oil.

Add salt and set aside.

Peel and wash the potatoes and cut into cubes.

Fry the potatoes in the olive oil until golden brown. Drain on kitchen paper. Serve with the spicy tomato sauce.

This is a traditional dish from Barcelona.

Tortilla (Spanish omelette)

Preparation time
15 minutes

Cooking time
30 minutes

Serves 4

Difficulty Easy

Ingredients

800g potatoes

8 eggs

1 onion, peeled and chopped

4 tablespoons olive oil

salt and pepper

Preparation

Peel and rinse the potatoes, dry them and cut them into slices ½ cm thick.

Heat 2 tablespoons of oil in a large pan, fry the onions and potatoes for 20 minutes, stirring often. The potatoes should be cooked.

Break the eggs into a large bowl, season with salt and pepper, then carefully stir in the potatoes and onion.

Heat the rest of the oil, pour in the egg mixture and cook the tortilla over a gentle heat for about 5 minutes. When the underside is golden brown, turn it over to cook the other side.

Serve hot.

Spain

Turning over the tortilla is a delicate operation. To make it easier, you can slide the frying pan into the oven, or you can put another hot and greased frying pan over the tortilla and turn both pans over at the same time.

Wrinkled potatoes with spicy mojo and green mojo
(Canary Islands)

Preparation time
30 minutes

Cooking time
20 minutes

Serves 4

Difficulty Easy

Ingredients

1 kg potatoes
250g salt

For the spicy mojo:
3 garlic cloves, crushed
1 teaspoon cumin
2 pickled green peppers, chopped
1 small hot chilli, seeded and finely chopped
120ml olive oil
2 tablespoons wine vinegar
salt

For the green mojo:
3 garlic cloves, crushed
1 teaspoon cumin
a large bunch of fresh coriander, chopped
12cl extra virgin olive oil
3 tablespoons vinegar

Spain

Preparation

To prepare the spicy mojo: Combine the garlic, chilli, peppers, cumin and salt. Mix in the oil and vinegar. Set aside.

To prepare the green mojo: Combine the garlic, coriander leaves and cumin. Mix in the oil and vinegar. Set aside.

To prepare the potatoes: Dissolve the salt in the water in a pan. Add the washed unpeeled potatoes, bring to the boil and leave to simmer for 20 minutes. Drain and leave on the heat for 5 minutes to dry so that a thin layer of salt forms on the potatoes. Serve immediately, accompanied by the mojos.

Alu tarkari

Preparation time
10 minutes

Cooking time
30 minutes

Serves 4 to 6

Difficulty Easy

Ingredients

800g potatoes

2 garlic cloves, peeled and finely chopped

1 onion, peeled and finely chopped

½ teaspoon sugar

1 tablespoon curry powder

2 tablespoons corn oil

salt

Preparation

Peel the potatoes and cut them into quarters.

Heat the oil in a frying pan and fry the onion and garlic until almost soft. Sprinkle the curry powder over and stir. Add the potatoes and enough water to cover them. Add the salt and sugar, stir well and cook over a low heat for about 20 minutes. Serve hot.

This dish can be served with chicken, or fish, or perfumed rice.

Suriname

Hasselback potatoes

Preparation time
30 minutes

Cooking time
1 hour 10 minutes

Serves 4

Difficulty Easy

Ingredients

1 kg potatoes
60g grated cheddar cheese
2 tablespoons breadcrumbs
2 tablespoons olive oil
40g butter
salt and pepper

Sweden

Preparation

Peel and wash potatoes, cut them in half lengthways.

Place a potato half on a work surface, cut side down. Place long-handled wooden spoons or chopsticks to prevent knife from cutting entirely through the potato as you make the slices. Cut the potato into thin slices accordion-style. Slice all the potatoes in the same way.

Preheat the oven to 160°C.

Arrange the potatoes in an oven dish.

Melt the butter, combine with the olive oil and brush over all the potatoes. Bake for 45 minutes, or until the potatoes are cooked, basting often with the butter and oil.

In a bowl mix together the breadcrumbs and cheddar. Sprinkle over the potatoes and bake for a further 10 minutes until golden brown.

Jansson's frestelse

Preparation time
15 minutes

Cooking time
55 minutes

Serves 4

Difficulty Easy

Ingredients

8 potatoes
3 onions, thinly sliced
16 anchovy fillets
100g butter
2 tablespoons vegetable oil
2 tablespoons breadcrumbs
250ml cream
120ml milk
salt and pepper

Preparation

In a pan heat 30g of the butter with the oil and fry onions until transparent.

Peel potatoes and cut into sticks about ½ cm thick and 4cm long. Rinse and dry them.

Butter an oven dish.

Arrange a layer of potatoes in the dish, cover with a layer of onions, season with pepper. Add the anchovies and finally a layer of potatoes.

Preheat the oven to 210°C.

Heat milk and cream, bring to the boil and pour over the potatoes.

Sprinkle breadcrumbs over the top and dot with the rest of the butter.

Bake for 45 minutes.

Serve hot.

Sweden

The dish is cooked once the potatoes have absorbed all the liquid.

Rarakor med graslok

Preparation time
10 minutes

Cooking time
20 minutes

Serves 4

Difficulty Medium

Ingredients

4 potatoes
4 tablespoons butter
4 tablespoons vegetable oil
½ bunch of chives, finely chopped
salt and freshly ground black pepper

Sweden

Preparation

Peel potatoes and grate them coarsely into a bowl.

Add chives, salt and pepper and mix well.

Heat butter and oil in a pan.

Put 2 tablespoons of potato mixture into the pan, flatten into a small pancake and cook for 3 minutes on each side until golden brown. Set aside and keep warm. Repeat with the rest of the mixture.

Potato strudel with horseradish sauce

Preparation time
30 minutes

Cooking time
50 minutes

Serves 4

Difficulty Medium

Ingredients

700g potatoes
4 onions, peeled and chopped
2 garlic cloves, peeled and chopped
100ml milk
1 egg
2 tablespoons thyme
1 bunch of flat leaf parsley, chopped
1 bunch of chives, chopped
1 tablespoon vegetable oil
4 sheets strudel pastry (or filo pastry)
50g butter, melted
salt, pepper, nutmeg

For the sauce:
1 apple
25g horseradish
1 plain creamy yoghurt
1 tablespoon nut oil

Preparation

Steam or boil the unpeeled potatoes for 25 minutes. Drain and peel them. Mash half the potatoes and cut the other half into small cubes.

Fry the onions and garlic in the vegetable oil.

Combine the mashed potatoes, milk, egg, onion and garlic, herbs, salt and pepper. Mix well and add the diced potatoes.

Place a sheet of strudel or filo pastry on a damp cloth and brush with some melted butter. Cover it with another sheet of pastry, brush with butter, and continue in the same way with the other 2 sheets of pastry.

Spoon the potatoes onto the upper sheet of pastry. Roll the strudel up with the help of the cloth, and fold in the ends.

Preheat the oven to 210°C.

Place the strudel in an oven dish. Brush the top with the rest of the butter. Cook in the oven for 25 minutes.

For the sauce: Combine the nut oil with the yoghurt and horseradish. Peel the apple, chop it into small cubes and add it to the sauce. Set the dish aside in the refrigerator until time to serve.

Switzerland

Raclette

Preparation time
10 minutes

Cooking time
55 minutes

Serves 4

Difficulty Easy

Ingredients

4 large potatoes
600g raclette cheese
20g butter
gherkins, pickled onions, pickles

Preparation

Scrub the potatoes and dry them. Wrap in aluminium foil and bake in the oven for about 45 minutes.

Remove the foil, cut a deep cross in each potato.

Cut the cheese into thin slices. Place the slices in the centre of the potatoes. Add a knob of butter on each and place under a hot grill for 10 minutes to melt the cheese.

Serve with gherkins, pickled onions and pickles.

Switzerland

This is a traditional winter dish in Switzerland and is highly appreciated by skiers.

Rösti

Preparation time
1 hour

Cooking time
55 minutes

Serves 4

Difficulty Easy

Ingredients
1 kg potatoes
4 tablespoons butter
salt and pepper

Preparation

The day before, steam or boil the unpeeled potatoes for 15 minutes. Drain and leave to cool.

On the day, peel potatoes, grate coarsely, sprinkle with salt and pepper.

Melt butter in a large pan. Add the grated potato, stir well so it is well covered with the butter. Cook over a medium heat for 20 minutes, stirring from time to time.

Flatten the potatoes in the pan to form a pancake. Cook over a high heat for 10 minutes to form a crust.

Turn the rösti over and cook the other side on a high heat for 5 minutes until golden brown. Slide on to a serving dish.

Switzerland

The potatoes should be half-cooked to make it easy to grate them.

Potato salad

Preparation time
10 minutes

Cooking time
25 minutes

Serves 4

Difficulty Easy

Ingredients

500g potatoes
1 onion, peeled and chopped
2 tomatoes
4 tablespoons olive oil
2 tablespoons lemon juice
1 tablespoon dried mint
4 sprigs of parsley, chopped
8 black olives

Preparation

Steam or boil the unpeeled potatoes for 25 minutes. Drain, peel and dice them. Place them in a salad bowl and drizzle with olive oil. Gently stir in the lemon juice and mint. Set aside to cool.

Wash and dry the tomatoes, remove the seeds and cut them into slices.

When the potatoes are cold, garnish with tomato slices and olives, and sprinkle with parsley.

Syrian Arab Republic

potato

Are sweet potatoes related to potatoes?

The sweet potato belongs to the plant family Convolvulaceae (the same family as morning glory) and is not a relative of the potato, which belongs to the Solanaceae (or nightshade) family (like eggplants and mandrakes).

The Spanish who brought sweet potatoes back from the West Indies called them by their native name "batatas". When white potatoes (papas) were introduced into Spain some years later, some people thought they were related. Soon papas were renamed patatas, but both were translated into English as potato.

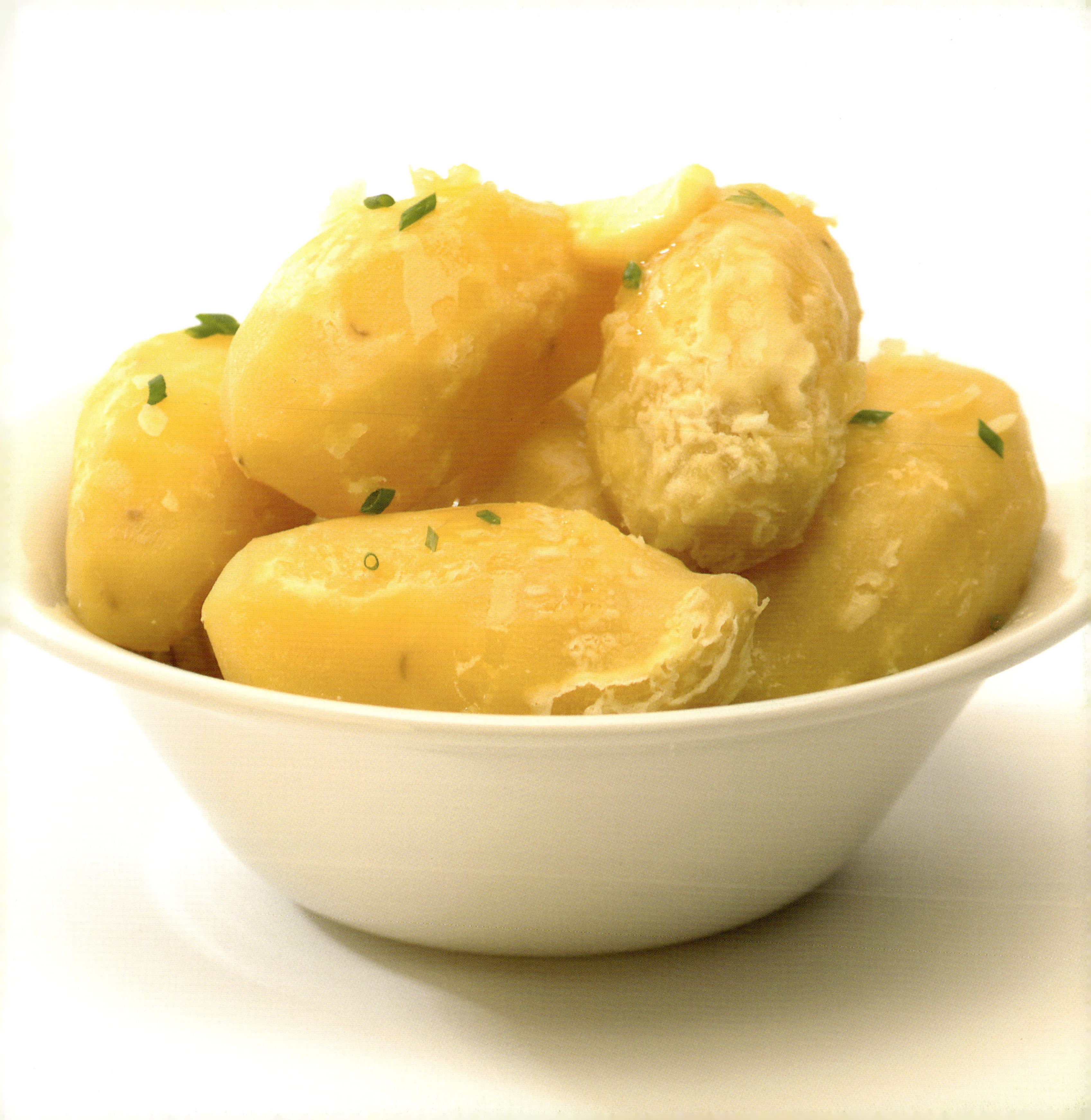

Thai potatoes

Preparation time
10 minutes

Cooking time
20 minutes

Serves 4

Difficulty Easy

Ingredients

400g potatoes
1 onion, peeled and chopped
½ cucumber, cut into thin sticks
1 lime
1 tablespoon nuoc-mâm
1 teaspoon brown sugar
½ teaspoon red chilli, seeded and chopped
150ml coconut milk
4 tablespoons unsalted peanuts, coarsely chopped
1 bunch fresh coriander, chopped

Preparation

Steam or boil the unpeeled potatoes for 20 minutes. Drain and set them aside to cool.

Grate the zest from the lime and squeeze out the juice.

Combine the lime juice and nuoc-mâm sauce with the brown sugar. Add the lime zest, onion, chilli and coconut milk.

Peel the potatoes, slice them into thin rounds and place them in a salad bowl. Add the cucumber and sauce. Stir together and garnish with coriander and peanuts.

Fatimajs fingers with tuna

Preparation time
20 minutes

Cooking time
30 minutes

Serves 4

Difficulty Easy

Ingredients

4 potatoes
1 onion, peeled and chopped
4 eggs
100g tuna, flaked
125ml oil
4 sheets brick dough or filo pastry
4 sprigs of parsley, chopped
salt and pepper

Preparation

Peel the potatoes, steam or cook them in boiling salted water until tender. Drain and mash.

Add the onion, parsley and tuna to the mashed potato.

Beat the eggs, season with salt and pepper.

Divide each sheet of filo pastry into two and lay them out on a work surface. Spoon the mash into the centre of each and roll them up.

Heat the oil in a large pan and fry them for a few minutes, drain on kitchen paper. Serve hot.

Tunisia

Potatoes with harissa

Preparation time
10 minutes

Cooking time
25 minutes

Serves 4

Difficulty Easy

Ingredients

800g potatoes
1 tablespoon harissa
1 tablespoon lemon juice
3 tablespoons olive oil
18 black olives

Preparation

Steam or boil the unpeeled potatoes for 25 minutes. Drain them and set aside to cool. When cool, peel and dice them.

Combine the harissa with the lemon juice and olive oil.

Put the potatoes in a serving bowl, add the olives and the dressing and mix carefully.

Spinach and potato borek

Preparation time
25 minutes

Cooking time
45 minutes

Serves 4

Difficulty Easy

Ingredients

4 potatoes
250g cooked spinach
1 onion, peeled and chopped
4 eggs
250ml milk
8 sheets of brick dough or filo pastry
3 tablespoons olive oil
salt and pepper

Preparation

Peel and wash the potatoes, dry thoroughly and grate.

Heat a tablespoon of oil in a large pan and fry the onion for 3 minutes. Add the potatoes and spinach, season with salt and pepper and continue cooking for 15 minutes. Remove from the heat. Beat 2 of the eggs and add them to the pan.

Whip together the milk, the 2 remaining eggs and the rest of the oil.

Preheat the oven to 180°C.

Open out the sheets of brick dough on a lightly floured work surface and brush them with the milk mixture. Arrange 4 sheets of pastry in a flan dish, spoon the vegetable mixture onto them, and cover with the remaining 4 sheets.

Fold in the edges of the pastry over the filling to form closed packages.

Cook in the oven for 25 minutes.

Turkey

Serve with a yoghurt sauce.

potato

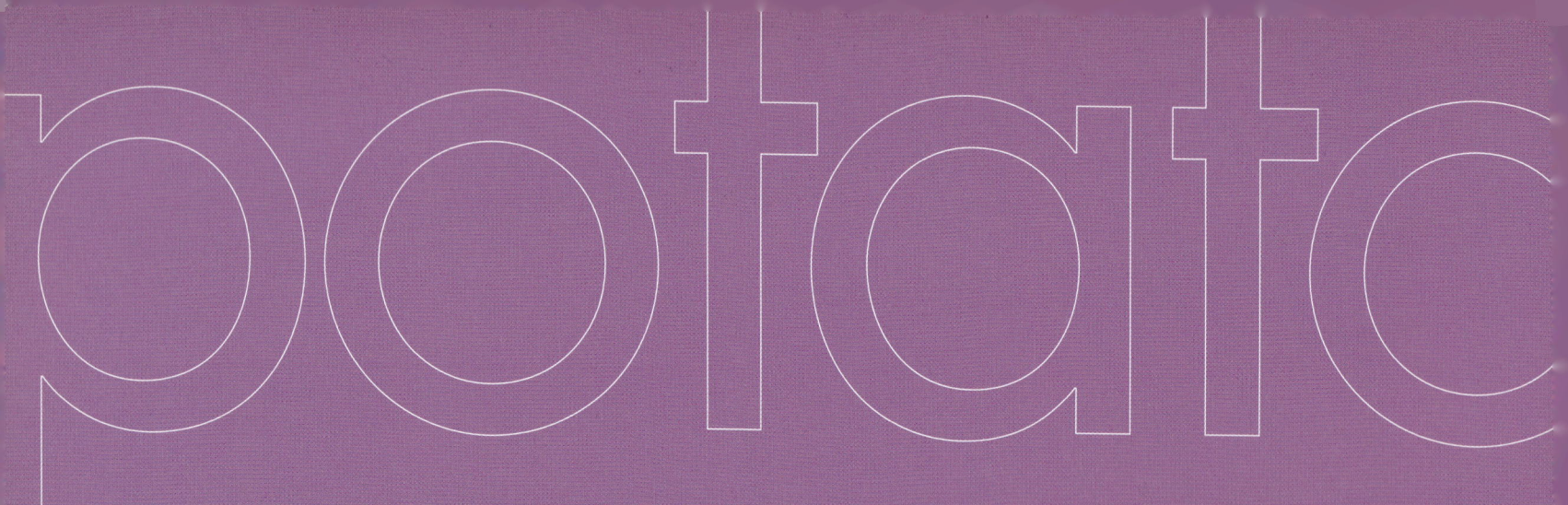

Do potato plants have flowers ?

It is surprising for many people that potato plants produce flowers — sometimes very attractive ones. They are usually white or mauve, but also sometimes blue, purple or deep violet. The fruits that grow from some varieties of potato plants resemble green cherry tomatoes, containing a lot of seeds. But don't try to eat them, they are not edible.

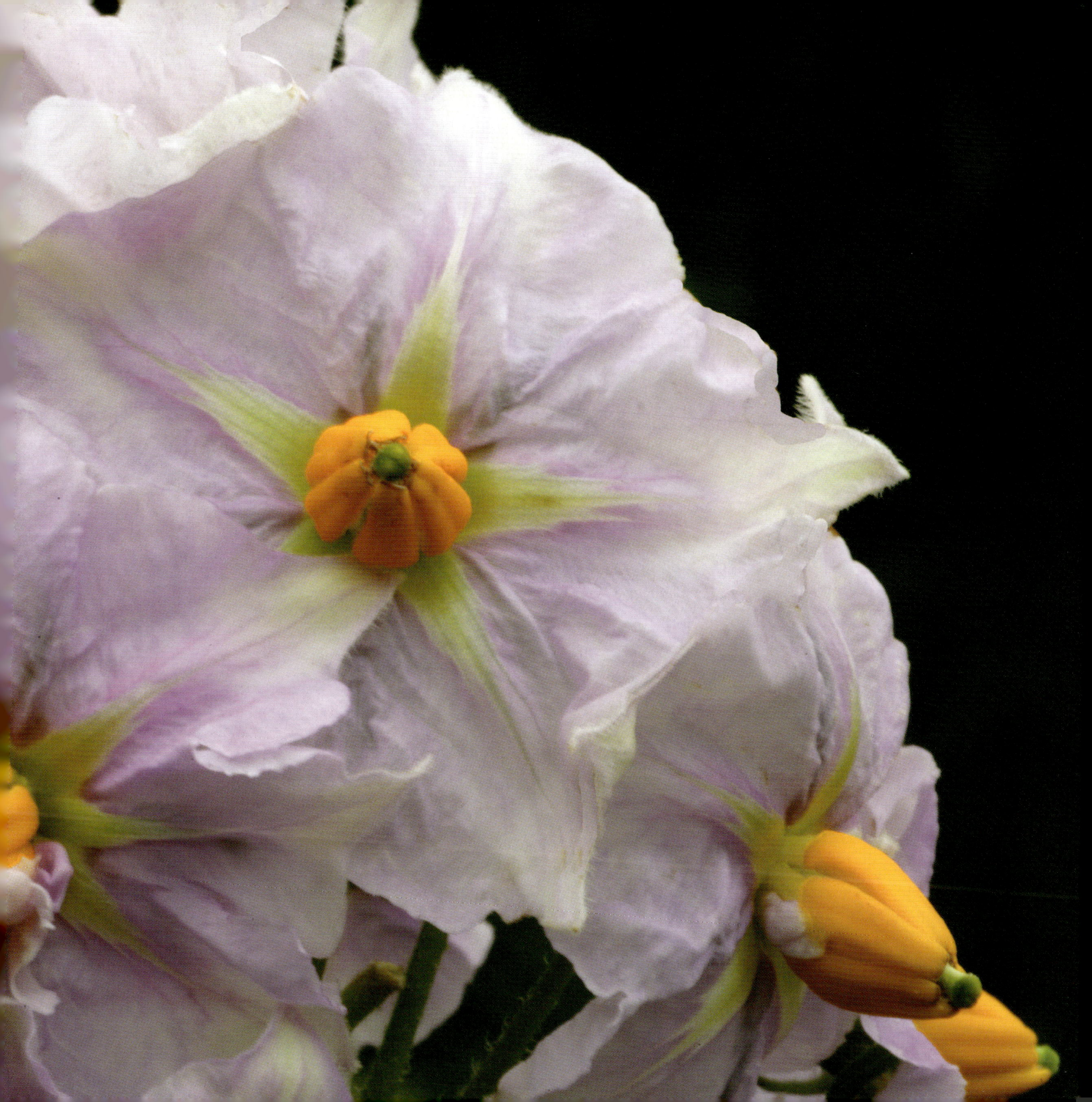

Potato soufflé

Preparation time
15 minutes

Cooking time
40 minutes

Serves 4

Difficulty Easy

Ingredients

500g potatoes
2 eggs, separated
125g cottage cheese
800ml cream
25g butter
salt

Ukraine

Preparation

Peel and dice the potatoes, steam or boil them for 25 minutes. Drain well and mash.

Beat the egg yolks and add to the potatoes, together with the cream, cottage cheese and a pinch of salt.

Whip the egg whites until they form stiff peaks. Fold them carefully into the potato mixture.

Preheat the oven to 210°C.

Transfer to a buttered gratin dish and bake for 15 minutes.

Serve immediately.

Bubble and squeak

Preparation time
10 minutes

Cooking time
30 minutes

Serves 4

Difficulty Easy

Ingredients

500g potatoes

250g green cabbage, sliced into fine strips

4 bacon slices, sliced into fine strips

1 onion, peeled and chopped

salt

Preparation

Cook the cabbage in salted water for 15 minutes, then drain.

Peel the potatoes, steam or cook in boiling salted water for 25 minutes. Drain and mash them.

Fry the bacon in a non-stick frying pan until crispy. Drain on kitchen paper.

In the same pan cook the onion until transparent. Add the potatoes, cabbage and bacon and mix together. Flatten the mixture in the pan to form a large thick pancake. Leave it to cook until golden brown on the underside. Turn it over gently onto a plate, slide it back into the pan and cook on the other side until golden brown.

Serve hot.

United Kingdom

This dish was traditionally made using leftovers, with cold cooked meat sometimes added.

Clapshot (Scotland)

United Kingdom

Preparation time
15 minutes

Cooking time
25 minutes

Serves 6

Difficulty Easy

Ingredients

600g potatoes
6 turnips
1 tablespoon whisky
salt and pepper

Preparation

Peel the potatoes and turnips, cook in separate pans in boiling salted water for 25 minutes.

Mash the vegetables together, season with salt and pepper. Stir in the whisky and serve hot.

This potato and turnip mash is traditionally eaten with haggis, a dish that the Scots eat at Hogmanay and on Burns Night (25 January) – in memory of Robert Burns, the eighteenth-century poet.

Roast potatoes (England)

Preparation time
10 minutes

Cooking time
1 hour 10 minutes

Serves 4

Difficulty Easy

Ingredients
8 medium potatoes
4 tablespoons olive oil

Preparation

Peel the potatoes and cut them in half lengthwise.

Steam or cook the potatoes in boiling salted water for about 20 minutes. Drain, dry them on kitchen paper and leave them to cool for 10 minutes.

Preheat the oven to 180°C. Lightly grease a baking sheet.

Using a fork make ridges in the potatoes. Place them on the baking sheet, cut side down.

Brush them with oil and bake in the oven for about 50 minutes. The potatoes should be golden brown and crispy.

Serve hot.

United Kingdom

Shepherd's pie

Preparation time
20 minutes

Cooking time
1 hour 10 minutes

Serves 6

Difficulty Easy

Ingredients

700g potatoes
700g cooked minced lamb
1 onion, peeled and chopped
1 teaspoon rosemary
100g butter
2 tablespoons flour
60ml hot stock
salt and pepper

United Kingdom

Preparation

Steam or boil the unpeeled potatoes for 25 minutes, peel and mash them.

Combine the meat, onion, rosemary, salt and pepper in a bowl.

Melt the butter in a pan, add the flour and cook for 3 minutes, then add the stock. Cook for 5 minutes stirring all the time. Add the meat mixture and mix well.

Preheat the oven to 180°C.

Spoon the meat mixture into an oven dish. Cover with the mashed potatoes. Cook for about 35 minutes.

Brabant timbale

Preparation time
25 minutes

Cooking time
30 minutes

Serves 4

Difficulty Medium

Ingredients

600g potatoes
6 small spring onions, chopped
2 garlic cloves, peeled and chopped
100g butter
60g parmesan cheese
4 sprigs of parsley, chopped
salt and pepper

Preparation

Line 4 cooking circles with greaseproof paper and place in a large gratin dish.

Combine garlic, onions, parsley, parmesan, butter, and a little salt and pepper.

Peel potatoes, rinse and dry well. Cut into thin slices.

Preheat the oven to 180°.

Put some potato slices in each cooking ring, cover with a spoonful of butter mixture, then a layer of potato. Continue until all ingredients are used up, ending with a layer of potatoes.

Cover with aluminium foil. Bake in the oven for 30 minutes.

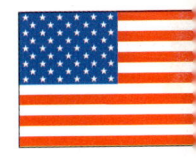

United States of America

This dish was created in Louisiana by a French settler.

Hash browns

Preparation time
10 minutes

Cooking time
30 minutes

Serves 4

Difficulty Easy

Ingredients

1 kg potatoes

1 onion, peeled and chopped

2 tablespoons fresh rosemary leaves

70g clarified butter

Preparation

Steam or boil the unpeeled potatoes for 20 minutes. Drain and set aside to cool.

Peel potatoes, cut into small cubes and place in a bowl with the onion, rosemary, salt and pepper. Mix together.

Heat $\frac{1}{3}$ of the clarified butter in a large pan. Place 4 cooking rings in the pan and fill each with potato, pressing the mixture down well with the back of a spoon.

Cook over a high heat, pressing them down often with a spatula, until golden brown on the underside. Turn over carefully to brown the other side. Drain on kitchen paper and keep warm while the other patties are cooking.

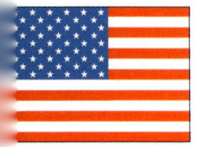

Serve hot.

In the United States, this dish is eaten for breakfast, lunch or dinner. Cooking circles are generally used in pastry making or for cooking poached eggs.

Mashed potato salad

Preparation time
15 minutes

Cooking time
25 minutes

Serves 6

Difficulty Easy

Ingredients

500g potatoes
2 stalks celery, washed, trimmed and finely chopped
1 onion, peeled and finely chopped
1 green pepper
250ml salad dressing
60ml milk
60ml vinegar
1 tablespoon mustard
1 tablespoon paprika
salt and pepper

Preparation

Steam or boil the unpeeled potatoes for 25 minutes. Drain, peel and mash in a large bowl. Add onion and celery.

In a separate bowl, combine milk, vinegar, salad dressing and mustard. Season with salt and pepper and pour over potatoes.

Wash the pepper, remove the seeds and cut into round slices. Garnish salad with pepper rings and sprinkle with paprika.

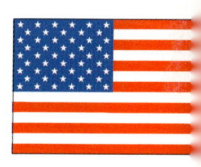

United States of America

Spicy potatoes with lemon

Preparation time
10 minutes

Cooking time
45 minutes

Serves 4

Difficulty Easy

Ingredients

4 large potatoes
2 lemons
2 red onions, peeled and chopped
8 garlic cloves
4 bay leaves
1 tablespoon tomato purée
1 teaspoon paprika
1 teaspoon dried oregano
1 teaspoon thyme
4 pinches of cayenne pepper
4 pinches of cumin
4 tablespoons olive oil
salt and pepper

Preparation

Wash the potatoes and cut them into quarters. Cut one lemon into pieces and squeeze the juice from the other.

Steam or cook the potatoes in boiling salted water for 5 minutes. Drain and arrange in an oven dish.

Add the pieces of lemon, the onions, unpeeled whole garlic cloves and bay leaves.

Preheat the oven to 210°C.

In a bowl combine the lemon juice with the tomato purée, olive oil, herbs and spices, salt and pepper. Pour over the potatoes and mix well. Bake in the oven for 40 minutes.

Serve hot.

United States of America

Vegetable and mashed potato gratin

Preparation time
20 minutes

Cooking time
1 hour 10 minutes

Serves 4

Difficulty Easy

Ingredients

700g potatoes
2 red peppers, seeded and chopped
2 onions, peeled and chopped
100g frozen peas
100g tinned sweetcorn
250g mozzarella
150ml cream
30g butter
2 tablespoons vegetable oil
salt and pepper

Preparation

Peel and wash the potatoes, dry and dice them. Steam or cook them in boiling salted water for 20 minutes. Drain and mash them. Add salt, pepper and butter.

Cook the peas in boiling salted water, then drain them.

Heat the oil in a pan and fry the onions and peppers. When they are tender, add the peas and sweetcorn. Cook for a few minutes. Season with salt and pepper. Add the cream and let it thicken over a medium heat.

Preheat the oven to 210°C.

Transfer the vegetables to a gratin dish. Cover them with mashed potatoes and top with the mozzarella cut into slices. Cook in the oven for 20 minutes.

Serve hot.

United States of America

The Incas had many uses for potatoes other than dinner. They placed raw slices on broken bones to promote healing. They carried potatoes in order to prevent indigestion. They even measured time with potatoes, by correlating units of time by how long it took to boil a potato.

Potato salad with peas and carrots

Preparation time 15 minutes

Cooking time 25 minutes

Serves 4

Difficulty Easy

Ingredients

1 kg potatoes
2 carrots, peeled and sliced
250g peas
60ml sour cream
60ml mayonnaise
4 sprigs of parsley, chopped
salt and pepper

Uruguay

Preparation

Cook the unpeeled potatoes, carrots and peas in separate pans. Drain them when cooked. Peel and dice the potatoes.

In a large bowl combine the mayonnaise with the sour cream, season with salt and pepper. Add the vegetables and mix together gently.

Garnish with parsley. Chill for 2 hours.

potato

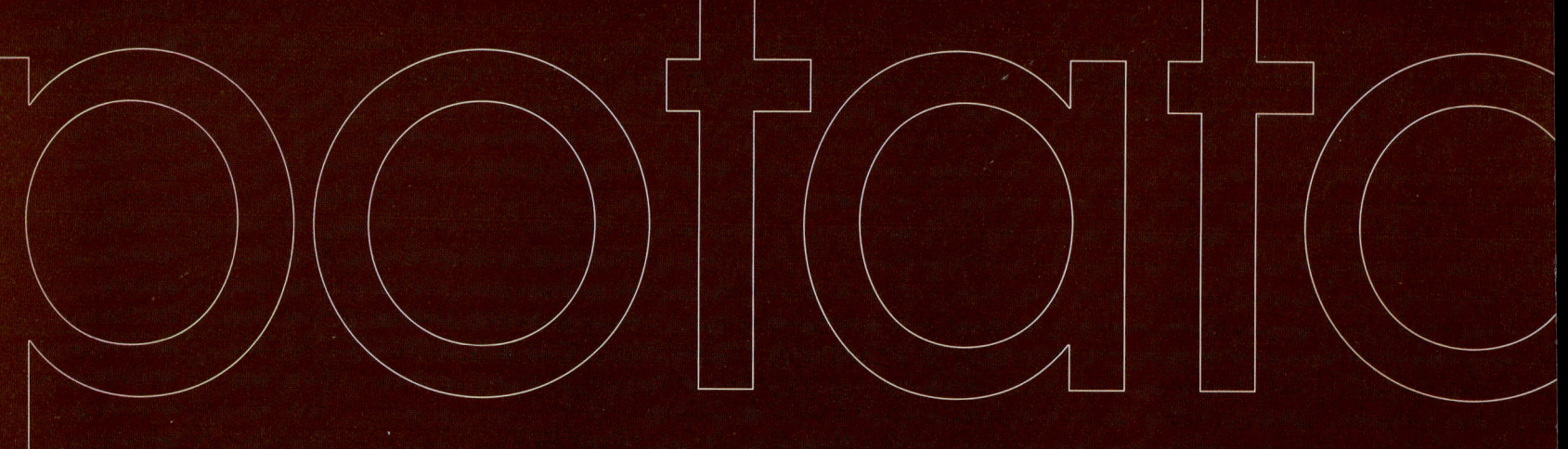

What is a potato worth?

During the Alaskan Klondike gold rush (1897-1898) potatoes were practically worth their weight in gold. Potatoes were so valued for their vitamin C content that miners traded gold for potatoes.

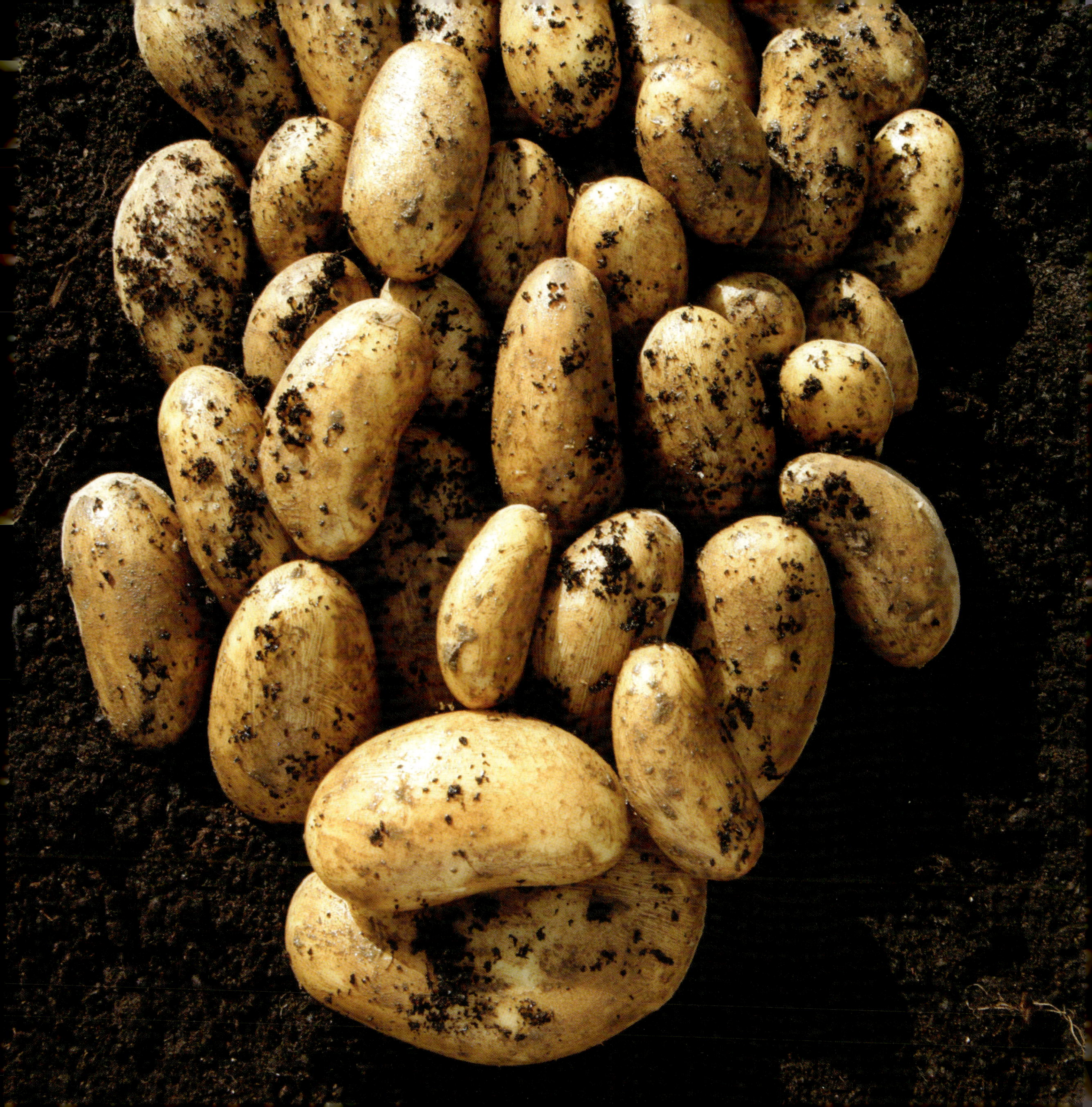

Sweet potato balls

Preparation time
15 minutes

Cooking time
40 minutes

Serves 4

Difficulty Easy

Ingredients

800g sweet potatoes
1 onion, peeled and chopped
600g fish
1 egg
6 tablespoons breadcrumbs
oil for deep frying
salt and pepper

Preparation

Cook the peeled sweet potatoes in boiling water for 30 minutes. Drain and mash them.

Poach the fish in boiling salted water, drain and flake the flesh.

Combine the sweet potatoes with the fish and onion, season with salt and pepper.

Beat the egg in a bowl, and put the breadcrumbs in another.

Using your hands form balls with the mash, dip each one into the beaten egg, then roll in the breadcrumbs.

Deep fry, then drain on kitchen paper.

Serve hot.

Vanuatu

Sweet potatoes with peanuts

Preparation time
15 minutes

Cooking time
35 minutes

Serves 4

Difficulty Easy

Ingredients

8 sweet potatoes
100g peanut flour
4 spring onions, finely chopped
4 tomatoes, seeded and chopped
¼ cabbage, finely chopped

Preparation

Peel the sweet potatoes and chop them into small pieces.

Heat the oil in a pan and fry the onions. Add the peanut flour and sweet potatoes. Mix together, cover with 200ml water and cook gently for 20 minutes.

Add the tomatoes and cabbage and continue cooking for 15 minutes.

Serve hot.

Vanuatu

Sancocho

Preparation time
30 minutes

Cooking time
1 hour 15 minutes

Serves 6

Difficulty Easy

Ingredients

400g sweet potatoes
1 chicken cut into pieces
500g veal shank
500g carrots
500g green bananas
400g pumpkin
400g tannia
3 onions
2 garlic cloves
salt and pepper

For the sauce:
300g tomatoes, skinned and chopped
2 onions, peeled and chopped
1 small hot chilli, chopped
2 tablespoons oil
500ml stock

Venezuela

Preparation

Peel all the vegetables.

Put the chicken pieces in a large pot with the veal shank, carrots, onions, garlic, salt and pepper. Cover with water and cook for 30 minutes. Add the bananas and tannia. Cook for another 20 minutes.

Add the sweet potatoes and cook for 15 minutes, then add the diced pumpkin. Cook for another 15 minutes.

To make the sauce: Fry the onions gently in the oil, add the tomatoes and chilli, cook over a low heat until reduced. Add the stock and cook for a further 10 minutes.

Drain the meat and vegetables, transfer to a serving dish.

Serve the sauce separately.

If you can't find green bananas, use yellow bananas that are barely ripe. Keep the cooking liquid; it makes delicious soup.

Contents

AFGHANISTAN
- Boranie katschalu 15
- Katschalu e joschdaada 16
- Khorme katschalu 17
- Pakavre katschalu 18

ALGERIA
- Potato patties with coriander 19
- Potatoes stuffed with sardines 20

ARGENTINA
- Ocro criollo 21
- Potato cake 22

ARMENIA
- Hachlama 23
- Potato keuftés 24
- Topic 25

AUSTRALIA
- Potato scallops 26

AUSTRIA
- Kartoffelsuppe 27
- Potato salad with radishes 28
- Salzburg potatoes 29

BELARUS
- Draniki 32
- Dratcena 33
- Kardoupliniki 37

BELGIUM
- Fried potatoes 35
- Liégeois potatoes 36
- Potato and bacon chicory 37
- Potatoes à l'ardennaise 38
- Stoemp with Brussels sprouts 39

BELIZE
- Sweet potato pudding 40

BOLIVIA
- Saltenas 41

BOSNIA (AND HERZEGOVINA)
- Pura 42

BRAZIL
- Potato and Jerusalem artichoke cream 43
- Salpicão facil 44

BULGARIA
- Patetnik 45
- Potato fritters with feta 46
- Potato salad 47

CAMEROON
- Potatoes with red beans 50

CANADA
- Potato and salmon salad 51
- Potatoes with cheddar 52
- Potato soup with dill 53
- Râpure 54
- Roasted cheese potatoes 55

CHAD
- Sweet potatoes with lemon butter 56

CHILE
- Charquican 57

CHINA
- Chinese potato salad 58

COLOMBIA
- Ajiaco 59
- Papas chorreadas 60
- Papas en azucar 61

CONGO
- Sweet potato stew 62

COSTA RICA
- Chayote 63

CÔTE D'IVOIRE
- Potato balls with spinach 64
- Sweet potato gratin 65

CROATIA
- Burek with potatoes 66

CUBA
- Sweet potato cake 67

CYPRUS
- Kleftiko 68

CZECH REPUBLIC
- Bohemian potato soup 69
- Potato gratin 70
- Potato quenelles 71

DENMARK
- Brændende kærlighed 74
- Caramel potatoes 75
- Curried potato salad 76

DOMINICA
- West Indian mash 77

DOMINICAN REPUBLIC
- Stewed turkey with potatoes 78

ECUADOR
- Lettuce and potato salad 82

EGYPT
- Khoudare belhalba 83
- Tagane batatesse 84

ESTONIA
- Meat stuffed potato pancakes 85
- Rosolje 86

ETHIOPIA
- Sweet potato and garlic soufflé .. 87

FINLAND
- Potato and herring casserole 90

FRANCE
- Aligot 91
- Bibeleskaes 92
- Gratin dauphinois 93
- Potato matelote 94
- Pâté bourbonnais 95
- Sarladais potatoes 96
- Soufflé potatoes 97
- Vichyssoise 98
- Zembrocal 99

GERMANY
- Bratkartoffel 102
- Knödel 103
- Potato salad 104
- Potato sausages 105

GREECE
Greek mash 106
Greek potato salad 107
Potato and vegetable briam 108
Potato patties with currants 109
Skordalia 110

GUATAMALA
Three-cheese potato gratin 111

HAITI
Sweet potato bread 114

HONDURAS
Honduran sopa 115

HUNGARY
Paprika potatoes 116
Potatoes with cheddar 117
Soup with potato balls 118

INDIA
Aloo gobi 122
Aloo tikka 123
Aubergine and potato curry 124
Potato green massala 125
Saag aloo 126

INDONESIA
Chicken and potato salad with satay sauce 127
Gado gado 128

IRAN
Pooreh seeb zamini 129

IRELAND
Champ 130
Colcannon 131
Dublin coddle 132
Irish stew 133
Potato scones 134

ISRAEL
Latkes 135
Potato ravioli 136

ITALY
Frittata 137
Potato gnocchi 138
Potatoes stuffed with mascarpone 139
Potatoes with artichokes 140
Tiella 141

JAMAICA
Spicy sweet potatoes 144

JAPAN
Shingjagaimo 145
Sweet potato croquettes 146

KENYA
Sweet potatoes with tomatoes 147

LATVIA
Livonian herrings 150

LEBANON
Herb potatoes 151
Potato stew 152
Potatoes in oil 153

LIBERIA
Sweet potato cake 154

LIBYAN ARAB JAMIHIRIYA
Tajin bel hut 155

LITHUANIA
Blynai is virtu bulviu 156
Cepelinai 157
Kugelis 158

LUXEMBOURG
Potato and sauerkraut pancakes 159

MADAGASCAR
Lasopy tongotr'omby 162

MALAWI
Mbatata cookies 163

MALTA
Patata l-Form 164

MAURITIUS
Potato dizef curry 165
Potato soup 166

MEXICO
Potato and bean salad 167
Stuffed potatoes 168

MOLDOVA
Potato soup with cheese 169
Pyrjoale 170

MONACO
Provençal tourtons 171

MONTENEGRO
Lamb with potato 172

MOROCCO
Maakouda 173
Potato tajine with onions and lemon 174

NETHERLANDS
Potato with bacon 178
Stamppot boerenkool 179

NIGERIA
Asaro 180

NORWAY
Baconbakte småpoteter 181
Potatoes with salmon 182
Salmon and potato pudding 183

PAKISTAN
Vegetable biryani 186

PARAGUAY
Naquis de batata 187

PERU
Cau cau 188
Ocopa 189
Papas à la huancaina 190
Papas rellenas 191

PHILIPPINES
Adobong gulay 192

POLAND
Kluski slaskie 193
Placki de Czesiu 194
Pyzy z miesem 195

PORTUGAL
Cod and shrimp gratin 196
Potatoes with cabbage 197
Potatoes with garlic cream 198

REPUBLIC OF KOREA
Korean potatoes 202

ROMANIA
Potato and ham fritters 203
Vegetable moussaka 204

RUSSIAN FEDERATION
Piroshki 205
Selyodka pod shouboy 206
Stuffed potatoes 207
Vegetable borsch 208

SENEGAL
Sweet potato jam 212

SERBIA
Potato pita 213

SLOVAKIA
Bramboraky 214
Halusky 215
Potato terrine with cèpes 216

SLOVENIA
Frika 217

SOUTH AFRICA
Potato salad with eggs 218
Potato stew 219

SPAIN
Aïoli potatoes 220
Cocido 221
Patatas bravas 222
Tortilla 223
Wrinkled potatoes with spicy mojo
    and green mojo 224

SURINAME
Alu tarkari 225

SWEDEN
Hasselback potatoes 226
Jansson's frestelse 227
Rarakor med graslok 228

SWITZERLAND
Potato strudel with horseradish sauce 229
Raclette 230
Rösti 231

SYRIAN ARAB REPUBLIC
Potato salad 232

THAILAND
Thai potatoes 236

TUNISIA
Fatimas fingers with tuna 237
Potatoes with harissa 238

TURKEY
Spinach and potato borek 239

UKRAINE
Potato soufflé 242

UNITED KINGDOM
Bubble and squeak 243
Clapshot 244
Roast potatoes 245
Shepherd's pie 246

UNITED STATES OF AMERICA
Brabant timbale 247
Hash browns 248
Mashed potato salad 249
Spicy potatoes with lemon 250
Vegetable and mashed potato gratin 251

URUGUAY
Potato salad with peas and carrots 252

VANUATU
Sweet potato balls 256
Sweet potatoes with peanuts 257

VENEZUELA
Sancocho 258